From The Hood To the Good

Surviving In a Foreign Environment

Sherry Styles

Create Your World

From The Hood
To The Good

Copyright © 1995, 2013, 2021 by Sherry Styles
Walking In Victory
P.O. BOX 501
DAYTON, OH 45405-0501

www.good-valuable-best.com

All scripture quotations, unless otherwise noted, are from the Holy Bible, King James Version.

All rights reserved. No part of this book may be reproduced or transmitted in any form or by any means without written permission from the author.
ISBN 978-0-9893736-0-9
Cover design William Pettiford, III, Dayton, OH
Photograph Cover by Noland Lester, Dayton, OH

Contents

Introduction - Surviving In a Foreign Environment 6
A Quantum Leap 8

I. Three Rules Of The Hood

    Rule 1 – Know Where You Are 11
        Don't Get Played on Know Know 11
        What You Don't Know *Can* Harm You..................... 15
    Rule 2 – Know Who You're Dealing With 17
        I'll Use It When I Need It 19
        The Little Sanctified Gal 21
    Rule 3 – Know How They Operate 23
        It's About Survival Baby! 26
        I Heard You The First Time 29
        Do It To Them Before They Do It To You 31

II. Confidence In God

    Put on The Whole Armor 34
    Seal The Deal 36
    Thanks For the Promotion 39
    Elevate – To the Next Level 39
    Experience – In God 41
    Exposure - To Kings 43
    Entry – The Open Door 45

III. Transitioning: From The Hood To The Good

    Mistaken Identity – I'm Gonna Be Me 49
    A Servant of The Most High God 51
    The Unwritten Rules 53

Have I Little Respect –I'm A Professional 56
Relax & Wear Your Jeans 57
Move To The Head of The Class 59
I'm On The Clock 61

IV. Walking in The Good

Walking in The Good 64
Don't Stop Dreaming 67
Awaken 68
Show 'Em Your Stuff 69
    Order in the House 69
    Opposition and My Pet Peeve 71
    Opposition and Elijah 74
    Outstanding Performance.. 75
    Overcome Obstacles and Win................................. 77
    Oh, I'm Prepared ! 78
Mind Your Manners 81
You Have A Better Idea 83
How You Play The Game – Walk In Authority 84
Integrity – Don't Compromise 87
Give Me My Mountain! 90
Walking In It! 96
A Strong Delusion 98
Raise the Bar 99
Dreams Don't Die, But They Do Take Time 102
The Test 104
Conclusion 106

What are people saying about From the Hood to the Good?

I Enjoyed Reading It!
        – Brenda Coleman, Troy, OH

I didn't just read your book. I studied your book!
        - Stanley, Dayton, OH

I really liked the reminder at the end.
        - Kyra, Dayton, OH

Introduction
From The Hood to the Good
Surviving In a Foreign Environment

Christina Evans and I were talking, standing in the vestibule at church. It's been a few years since the conversation, maybe about 15. We were discussing our work experiences and careers, just a casual conversation. Before I could grasp what was happening, I spoke three survival tips to succeed in a work environment. I told her, *"Honey, you better know where you are, know who you're dealing with, and know how they operate."* She said, *"That's good, I'll have to remember that Sherry,"* as her eyes lighted up she took notice of the words I spoke. I agreed. I'd never said this before. A light bulb flashed in my mind and I knew it was Him speaking. Then I confirmed, *"When God gives you something, you know its God. One day I'll do something with that!"* We both smiled a big smile and she nodded in agreement. *"You really should,"* she said.

I'd been living this way: Understanding where I am, who I'm dealing with in that environment, and knowing how they operate. Not taking time to write it down, I just did it. Day-to-day I worked with people who functioned differently than me, and usually I was successful in working with others.

These tips worked 15 years ago and they still help me today. *I don't mind sharing valuable information that will help someone gain confidence to make a transition in a work environment and honestly, any other environment.*

God said, *"Now is the time to give what I've given to you. Share how you maintained your own unique personality and still had the respect of co-workers, supervisors, CEO's, and foreign dignitaries."*

He gave me the Good to help me make it. That's what I've chosen to call these inspired words, the Good. The Hood is the place where I lived and resided, but it's not who I am. We often associate the Hood with a negative influence and a negative outcome, but greatness does come forth from the Hood. The Good has always been within me waiting to break forth! The Good is waiting to break forth in you too and you'll find out you don't have to settle for that negative image projected on those who live in the Hood. Don't adopt your environment and surroundings as who you are, or to define your personality. There's a greater treasure on the inside of you, and *you* control your destiny – Now it's time to allow the Good to shine through you.

The three principles are so simple that you don't have to remember a lot for application, yet strong enough for you to know you can survive in an environment that is foreign to you without losing your cool. At the end I'll give you a reminder that will reinforce everything we discuss.

A Quantum Leap

Let us take a leap into your future and start clapping now for the Victory you want to achieve. Just by picking up this motivational jewel you have taken a step to achieve ultimate success in life. So take a few moments to lift yourself higher as you think of the investment you made that will reap bountiful benefits. Don't be afraid to look at yourself to see who you really are. Once you do, you can see what steps are necessary for fulfillment of your destiny.

I have a message for you, enclosed in these inspirational pages. In order to relay this simple message I've changed the names of people and places but the characters are true. The message is - *"You are some one Special!"* Your surroundings or circumstances do not determine who you are. What determines who you are is totally up to you and lies within. I declare: *What God has to say about you is important. He has the final say. I declare His image of you in your life right now - He knows the real you.*

I was born in a town where many talented artists have their roots. Famous vocalists and singing groups, artists, writers, television personalities, actors, and actresses started in my small city. Many of them have taken their talents and blessed others, even worldwide. They have humble roots, just wanting to allow the real person within to shine.

My roots are humble too. Yet there's something that sets us apart and unites us: I've been dreaming. Dreaming cannot be taken away from you or me. You have a great destiny if you will dare to dream. All excuses for failure have been eradicated and now is the time to create the success that you hope for. Allow your dreams to direct you to a bright future.

When studying the history of great men and women you will see a unique trend. Their dreams superseded poverty, low self-esteem and failures.

Their motivation to fulfill a dream and achieve greatness propelled them forward as they pressed past the obstacles on the road to great achievement. Some did a quantum leap and leaped so far ahead that people are still wondering what happened and how they achieved such greatness. People such as Michael Jackson, Quincy Jones, Oprah Winfrey, Shirley Caesar, and many others, moved beyond normal expectations. Their unique talents impress the world!

There is a key to success and it begins with the one who gives life, Jesus Christ! With him leading and guiding your pathway, you can fulfill a destiny you never imagined. Fulfilling your dreams is only a few pages away. I want to help you reach your utmost potential. You have the key to success. You just need to use the key and unlock it!

Congratulations on your destiny, it's just moments away. I say with assurance, the Creator is hiding in you and he's waiting to birth that dream into reality. It starts with acknowledging him. Take a few moments to thank him right now.

Three Rules Of the Hood

Rule 1 – Know Where You Are
Don't be played - Know, Know, Know

Everyone I grew up with knew how to survive in the neighborhood. Such as that family in the bright green house, we knew what they were about. They had a special *unique* business and people were drawn to their house by its outlandish green color. My mother did not encourage me hanging out over there with that business going on. I had a different perspective on life anyway, so it wasn't a problem for me to spend a lot of time there. I learned how to survive my own way.

In the Hood you keep your eyes open, by knowing who has a big mouth, and who you should and shouldn't tell your business to. In the Hood you can't hang out with everyone. In the Hood you have to know what's going on in your neighborhood to survive it, or you will be taken advantage of. This is true of any neighborhood, but it's especially true a neighborhood with certain activities governing its existence.

Mom warned us about those really "out there" kids, the troublemakers, and she told us to keep a distance for our own safety. (After a while you could see why, their lives were on a pathway to destruction.) The rules weren't too difficult to follow especially if we listened and paid attention to what was happening. Word on the street travels faster than any newscast I ever heard, so when parents give instructions its best to listen, because they are in tune to their surroundings for your sake.

Parents have a built-in radar to detect practically anything that could harm their children. They must keep a watch out so they talk to their children about life to keep them safe from harm. They send little messages that instill values for living and living well. Parenthood is a big responsibility and it takes so much to keep children on the correct path these days. A standing ovation is due to the parents who succeed in parenting and don't have to bail a child out of jail. And even if a child goes to jail, once children make it to adulthood and become citizens who they can be proud of, it is outstanding. With *all* the responsibilities of parenthood it's easy to omit information and that's what I want to share.

To make a long story a short one, my parents missed a few pointers I needed to know when I entered into the work force. They told me how to survive the Hood where we lived, but with all the responsibilities of parenthood, they didn't tell me about the world of work.

When it comes to the world of work, you have to see some things for yourself and govern yourself accordingly no matter how much your parents share with you. Parents do their best to get you through school and to get you employed to support yourself. It takes so much just to accomplish that! With every effort to push me out the door to my first job, my parents missed a few important factors. Once I left my home environment and began to experience life outside of it, I learned three powerful keys to survive from the minute I walked outside the door. . . so here we go.

The first tool is to *Know Where You Are.* Ask yourself the question *Where am I?* and think about it. What's the history of this place? Who started the company, who's been in charge? Do your homework and find out about the environment. Adopt the culture and understand why this place exists. Who is in charge now? Thinking about *Where You Are* changes your perspective.

There are times you'll have to remind yourself *Where You Are* because it's different from your way of thinking and operating, especially if you're from the Hood. I noticed there were only a few people like me in my work environment, only a few people with the same cultural background and values. And so, I asked people like me why it was that way. I knew they understood because they were employed here a while. I could not understand some differences and some differences I understood well. I understood who was in charge I just did not understand why it was that way. It's best to listen to those that know history, what could it hurt to listen? We're on earth to learn and to grow. I am a poor soul if I maintain the mentality of the Hood all my life when there is so much life to be lived.

Where am I?

I'm sitting here at this company, a place where the value statement is to produce quality. People are here for the same reason I am, to earn a decent living, but their motivation is different. Many have been taught to get over the best way they can. You are superior because of your race, class, cultural background, who you know, etc. But my morals and values are quite different. I was taught to love others no matter who it is. I'm so glad for this teaching; it allows me to see people clearly for who they are, not looking through rose colored glasses, and certainly not thinking that because of those things I mentioned above that I am in some ways better or superior.

At the previous company I worked for, I was accustomed to moving at the speed of light. It was a fast-paced environment that required a fast tempo to get the job done. It was like driving 100 miles a minute in a 50 mile zone, so I had to make a major adjustment at this new company. It was a different world. That's all I knew until that door closed and I found employment elsewhere, where I am writing this from today. In this new environment the speed is 25 miles a minute and I'm still moving at the speed of light. My mind races to get things done. My body follows this flow of thinking and I find myself moving quickly, with others around me just looking at me wondering what my problem is (she'll catch on). This is where I am – Now.

What an adjustment. It may have taken me a year, I can't pinpoint it. All I know is - I had to make the adjustment. The adjustment was necessary because I'm in a different place now. I've moved across town to the suburbs, a nice area where everything is state-of-the art, the best. The roads are nice and repaired instantly when damage occurs. Problems are handled immediately to avoid a disruption of a nice life style they've chosen to live. Residents and co-workers drive the latest cars, live in fine houses, send their kids to the best of schools, and eat out at least twice a week. It's not like that in the Hood where residents drive a car until it falls apart, are apartment dwellers, their kids attend public school, and may have to settle for a meal they can get. Problems are handled when the resources are available, and there are limited lifestyle options. The image is quite different and I don't mind. The difference is like night and day. *I know where I am.*

As I go to work every day I am reminded of these differences and I learn to adapt to the procedures and methods that are followed in accomplishing even the smallest tasks. The mindset is different and I must know where I am at all times to effectively work in this environment. From the Hood, to a fast-paced environment, then to a slow-paced environment, I have to ask myself, *Where Am I?*

What You don't know CAN harm you (The inside Scoop)

The old cliché' *"What you don't know can't harm you,"* is far from the truth! Actually the opposite of what we're told is true. In my few years of working with people, I've learned that if you don't know what's happening around you, it's possible to miss out on the greatest blessings. It is important to *stay in tuned to God.* He's got the inside scoop on every event and everybody. And because of his sovereignty, he can tell you what's happening in places that others may not have knowledge of yet.

He did this for the prophet Elijah. (1 Kings 6: 8-23) When Syrian's army planned an attack, the prophet informed the Israelites. With this inside connection, the Syrians' plans fell through and the Israelites escaped capture. This upset the Syrians many times because they failed to prevail over Israel. God will always make a way for his people. God will always stand up for his people. God's people are those who walk closely with him and are doing his will, those who spend time with him and seek his face, those who have his spirit on the inside, and those who read his Word and put their belief and trust in Him. When walking close to him you already have the victory and He shows you how to obtain it.

There was plenty that I did not know and was unaware of about life, but in my prayer life God opened my eyes to the plots that were planned and made a way of escape for me. He led me to good things too. I have examples of things God told me to do that kept my back. I walked victoriously because my prayer life kept me aware of how to avoid pitfalls, traps, and things to cause me to stumble. Many days God allowed me to see the spirit of a person and what their true intent was at that moment. Of course I did not hold grudges when their purpose was revealed to me. We must always understand that the devil uses people at a moments notice to get to you. So you can't keep them in bondage. Recognize that it's him using them, Praize God for the Victory and Keep on Movin!

I'll share one example of how God kept my back. I learned from a teacher that you must always protect yourself. I had reports to submit and I always kept a separate file hidden from view of anyone and unknown to anyone but me. This one time I turned in a monthly report to my supervisor, who said she never received it. I could see by the look in her eyes that she thought she had me. Now, I honestly don't know why it never reached her hands, but I saw the look of surprise in her eyes when I returned with a copy of the report. My handy file saved me that day! God has given me insight on how to stay ahead of the game. Bless his name!

Rule 2 – Know Who You're Dealing With

Look around you. Do you *Know Who You're Dealing With?* Who are the people working there? What are their values, morals, and agenda? Are they family or career oriented? What are their priorities according to their culture? That's what you'll have to work in, not your own culture. Be careful here, unless it's someone just like you owns the business, someone with your same values, cultural background, and morals. You will have to adopt the culture of those in charge while you're there. For eight hours you will work with rules or a set of beliefs that may be foreign to you. Your survival is dependent upon you knowing as much about it as possible.

Know Who You're Dealing With?

This is where it gets tricky. The people you work with could be ever so nice, and ever so treacherous. Hmm... There's something behind that cheesy grin. Hmm... If you've been taught to love, they may have been taught to cheat or to get over the best way they can and trample over you in the process.

My mother and father always demonstrated God's love to us. They gave to others. They had friends everywhere and always gave us life statements to keep us on the right track and it worked. Their friends were of different races and cultures too. But the people I worked with knew not of this love. Their hearts were cold. They judged by your skin color no matter how you conduct yourself. What a pity, this perception prevents them from showing equality to everyone.

Coinciding with *Knowing Who You're Dealing With* you must *Know Yourself*. Where you live does not define who you are. My grandmother lived in the south. She had a queen's mind and she never settled for less than the best. Her education was minimal compared to today's opportunity to attain an education. She was a Godly woman and her schooling with Him far exceeded anything I ever learned in a book or was taught by people I worked with. I'm glad to have these roots because I know the difference in what matters and what doesn't, what's real and what's fake. I am blessed! It's who I am.

What you put on the inside of you must come forth and it will, whether or not you want it to. But how? The apostle Paul tells us how to deal with others in their environment for we have a purpose as ambassadors for Christ:

> *"For though I be free from all men, yet have I made myself servant unto all, that I might gain the more. And unto the Jews I became as a Jew, that I might gain the Jews. . . To the weak became I as weak, that I might gain the weak: I am made all things to all men, that I might by all means save some. . ."* (1 Corinthians 9: 19-23)

Survival in a company or kingdom has a requirement. Preparation. Once you equip yourself with knowledge of the people of the company or kingdom, you can mesh with them successfully and smile about it. Only then can you know *Who You're Dealing With*. At that point you'll understand their motivation, how to conduct yourself, and even what behavior is appropriate and acceptable. Preparation is the key to success while you're there.

Do your homework and pay attention, you must *Know Who You're Dealing With*.

I'll Use It When I Need It

When I was a child I learned about God. I learned about the bible. I found out many people learn about God too, but all do not view their teachings with the same interest or fervency. I need him everyday! I found out things go better with Christ! When He's first, my results are a lot better than if I leave him out. I've actually noted the differences and any born again believer will tell you the same. I can't afford not to have his daily input.

Others can take him or leave him, only calling on him when things don't go as expected. He's just knowledge they've gained over the years. (That's how they think) So when someone speaks of how good he is, they don't understand the concept of having God in everything.

There's a vast difference in knowing about someone and knowing someone. As you daily spend time with a person you come to know the individual. You understand how they think, what their limitations are, the character they possess, what they will and won't do. When you read what someone else has said about a person, you know *of them*. That's a second hand account of the character they possess.

The results of interacting with Him everyday are amazing. A person who has joy no matter what's going on, a good attitude in tough times (you can verify it), and doesn't allow any one, any circumstance, or any problem get to them is worth consideration. In this life everybody I know has problems and unfavorable circumstances at some time. So how do you make it through? The person with continuous joy obviously has a connection worth checking into. Alcohol and other substances provide temporary satisfaction, but the problems remain unsolved when the high is over. They leave bad side effects too. *Do I need God - every day?* Maybe it depends upon the side effects.

People in certain cultures only look to God when they need him, when it's something they can't handle, i.e. money ran out, sick with cancer, spouse left them. Sometimes they even blame Him. The truth is - I don't call Him when I need him. I love him and He's a part of my everyday life. In a work environment be careful to recognize everyone may not adhere the need for God like that, but it shouldn't change you. I am reminded of an old proverb.

"In all thy ways acknowledge him and he shall direct thy path."
(Proverbs 3: 6)

The *Little Sanctified Gal*

I did not realize how much attention you gain from others once you declare you're saved and living for Jesus. As a quiet person standing a head above most others, I am always surprised when I get attention. As I was growing up, the people with money and connections were most popular, were asked to participate most often, and were given first chance at different activities. I attended the high school with "all the ladies" (one male friend of mine told me this), but I didn't have all the right clothes, many boyfriends, and wasn't popular at all. I didn't make the best dressed list and wasn't noticed like "all the ladies" because I didn't have much.

In retrospect, one interest helped my popularity, track & field. Oh yes, I loved to run. It gave me a little exposure and it was fun, but I still wasn't noticed like "all the ladies." Track was introduced to me through my daddy. He took my brother and me to Welcome stadium where we participated and earned a few medals. This showed me the power of influence. When my dad took time with family it made a difference, and my introduction to track & field at an early age proved helpful to me in high school.

One day after I graduated from high school, I found out people noticed me. I visited my cousins' father just to check on him one summer day. He's an older man from the south. He called me *"the Little Sanctified Gal"* with his southern twang that made me laugh. His words *"the little sanctified gal"* surprised me. Although I had few dealings with him, he knew enough to notice me. This was a compliment, because it says that I was set apart for God's use and he knew that. That's what sanctified means, set apart.

During that visit, he told me a lot about people and life that I knew nothing of. Words that help me even to this day. Even though I lived in the

Hood, I believed more things I was told than I should have and that's not good. I was naïve in my understanding. He perceived my knowledge of life was limited, and God was protecting me. He was right. I needed all the information he shared. The problem is, I didn't know my life was so limited. Everyone knew that I was saved but I didn't know my salvation experience attracted their attention. Popular now, me? Didn't know til I talked to him. It was a revelation, this name he called me. I found out others really know if you're living the life you speak of. They take notice of you. I knew the Word of God, but had much to learn about people. This changed soon enough for me.

Even in the work environment, people know who you are without placing a banner across your forehead or wearing a t-shirt. Then it's nice to know others appreciate Him too.

Rule 3 – Know How They Operate

You've taken note of *Where You Are* and *Who You're Dealing With*. Now to fully understand and adapt to the environment you must *Know How They Operate*. This is the most difficult rule to accept and adjust to. The underlying reason is others may operate under a different set of rules than you're accustomed to.

Many times I've wanted God's Golden Rule to govern those around me:

> *"And as you would that men should do to you, do you also to them likewise"* (St. Luke 6: 31)

Eventually I realized his rule governed *me* in order to handle where I was. Of all the commandments, this one puts me in check the quickest. It implies consequences to *my* actions. Good consequences and bad consequences. This gives me the opportunity to set the environment around me. I am governed by my own actions and by adopting this principle, I free myself of any wrong doing and open the door for God to bless me. I am at peace with myself and with others, acting with the best interests of everyone involved at heart with no harm to anyone.

It simply means *"Do unto others as you would have others do unto you."* In the Hood it takes on an *umm...mm, well...* slightly different meaning *"Do it to others, before they do it to you."* **Now be careful with that!** The wrong attitude could cause serious damage to all involved. God can never bless you or have your back when you have that Hood attitude and mentality. Then he would have to erase Paul's letter to the Galatians when he told them (and his word is unchangeable):

"Be not deceived; God Is not mocked; for whatsoever a man soweth, that shall he also reap" (Galatians 6: 7)

This scripture has a two-fold meaning. To *sow*[1] is to scatter (seed) over land, earth, for growth or to plant. To *reap*[2] is to gather or take a crop or harvest or to get as a return, recompense, or result. When you plant love, love with grow and return to you at harvest time. When you plant evil, evil will grow and return to you at harvest time. Walking in the Golden Rule sets an atmosphere of who God is in you and who you are in God. He operates in Love even for our enemy's sake. Even when they oppose you, he loves them as you should.

Any time a child of God behaves outside of his guidelines (His Word) it's mocking him and making him appear as one who is unlearned. So he places us in adverse situations to verify what rule we govern ourselves by.

When you face adversity it motivates you to think of the outcome you want, and the Golden Rule will come before you. The Word motivates you to consult God and to act with him on your side versus reacting from the Hood's perspective with learned behavior. One reaction is positive, the other reaction is negative.

Countless times I wanted my supervisor at work to be fair, when ultimately he/she suited their own purposes by unwritten rules. Clearly they were not motivated with the same values and operated according to their own rules. Therefore, their method of operation was foreign to me.

Their methods were not foreign to God. Long ago he covered his followers with a sure-proof method of wining every battle. He made provisions to govern me to walk victoriously with the Golden Rule. I tried

---

[1] Flexner, Stuart B., Editor Random House College Dictionary, Revised Edition
[2] IBID

his method with the right motivations, with the right attitude and spirit, and was assured victory every time. *How They Operate* was different and I learned the consequences were different too. My resolution was to treat everyone with the same kindness I wanted in return.

Now I *Know How They Operate*. I understand how things are done in that culture and what rules they are governed by. I'll explain in more detail in the following pages.

It's About Survival Baby!

In a courtroom the bailiff swears in a person on the witness stand by saying, *"Do you swear to tell the truth, the whole truth, and nothing but the truth, so help you God? What you say can and will be used against you in a court of law."* The witness responds with, *"Yes"* or *"I affirm."* I'm here to tell you *"what you say, can, and will be used against you."* That's what they say in a court of law and you better know it's true in the work place.

Every day I enter the work force, I expect to have a great day with no drama. I seek to be at peace with every person I encounter. I am there to be a positive support and team member. My purpose for working is to earn an income for a job well done and to enjoy the job I perform. It is God's light, his love that's at work, and a positive work ethic.

People with a different motivation can be intimidated by a quiet peaceable personality. Often people see that light and seek to put it out, or to make it dim. Light motivates change. Our senses alert us that when a light shines - everything starts moving. God's light shining exposes the darkness surrounding it. No one wants their darkness exposed including those without God's light who don't want change. So those who are intimidated by that light are on guard, run for cover, and find accusations to put out that light.

So watch what you say. Words are very important and can be used to entrap you. Always remember, everyone around may not understand you and are not for you, but always know that God is!

"What shall we then say to these things? If God be for us, who can be against us" (Romans 8:31)

I've learned to keep my mouth shut especially when I want to speak up the most. Let me rephrase that, I've learned to watch what I say and choose my words carefully. Opposors hang on to your every word. Some, to make sure you represent the truth you speak of- because they're seeking a better way. Others, to hang you by your words - because they're running from the right way. In a world where others believe the words of PT Barnum, *"There's a sucker born every minute,"* you better know who is around you and their motives. It doesn't take long to find them out. People who operate by PT Barnum's rule will trample over you and think nothing of it.

Jesus said, *"Not every one that saith unto me, Lord, Lord shall enter into the kingdom of heaven."* (St. Matthew 7: 21) Everyone that says your name, and smiles isn't for you, therefore, make an effort to win them to Christ and in turn win them on your side. Get them working for God and they'll work for you and with you. This is important because we become our best selves when He is in charge! Let them know that God loves them and that's where the great light they see comes from. After all, you've been transformed from darkness to light and they can make that transformation too. He loves us all the same. There's no respect of persons with God.

Watch your words! You cannot give the enemy an excuse to hang you by them. Your enemy is not the person you're working with, but a higher power that doesn't want anyone to succeed. Believe me, he doesn't want to lose any souls so he's looking for an opportunity to make a spectacle of you by the what you say and by your behavior. Don't give up too much information - it could be to your harm. Hezekiah (Isaiah 38, 39) did this after receiving a great blessing. He exposed things he should have held dear to his heart. It's all about Survival Baby! Words never spoken can't be traced. Watch your mouth and God'll watch your back. When you speak it is community knowledge or common knowledge. It's what you say to all and there is safety in being honest to everyone with the same information.

Many people ask questions. They want to know who you are, where you came from, why you're here, and what motivates you. It's in your best interests to speak well of every person you meet and you can do it. But do not give an enemy any ground against you. So watch it when a person is asking too many questions. It's not common knowledge to them, it's ammunition to bring your destruction. Just imply nod your head and listen.

It's all about Survival Baby!

I Heard You the First Time

God has a way of causing your senses to awaken and become alert. He knows when you operate by rules of the Hood, and when your mentality needs adjusting so he sends messages. He uses leaders as his spokesperson.

Some leaders understand how to communicate a message with effectiveness. Others have a misperception about those in the Hood. They believe you cannot hear well, or are not paying attention, and repeat their words for that reason. You're not ignorant as you're perceived to be and this misperception weakens your ability to adhere and move forward. Your senses become dull and it keeps you in bondage. When a message is repetitive, either the sender is trying to reinforce the message or he doesn't recognize the hearers' ability to comprehend the message. This is obviously true when you notice it exercised over and over again. Let me explain further.

If the sender speaks quickly and there's limited time for the receiver to clearly hear or comprehend the words, it is quite different from a sender who speaks in a manner to imply the receiver doesn't have the mentality to understand what's being said. Therefore the statements are repeated over and over until the person gets it.

We are bombarded with so much information that a message must be expressed with correct articulation and emphasis to remain in our hearts and mind. In communication whether interpersonal, business, or any spectrum, the sender has a message to communicate. He selects a method the receiver understands and is quick to adhere to for effectiveness. At times a message needs repeating to bring clarity, for reinforcement, and to block out the friction between the sender and receiver. So it's alright to repeat the message – sometimes. But we have to become good hearers.

In the workplace an employee gets one opportunity to hear what's being said. Leaders don't want a lot of questions afterwards, unless the message was unclear when first spoken. A supervisor will not repeat instructions. Their rationale is they don't have time. An employee is expected to listen at all times and be alert. And it's their own problem if they miss it. Don't become dull in your hearing. When vital information is imparted – don't miss it. Stay alert.

I learned to listen and to stay alert because my supervisor had the wrong perception of me. He expected me to react a certain way and by failing to respond in that manner, he assumed I was hard of hearing or simply do not understand.

I was given an assignment and moved quickly to achieve it. The problem arose when he thought I wasn't smart enough to perform the job without his direct guidance and input. He returned to tell me a second time to perform the same function. To his surprise, I'd already successfully complete the assignment and presented him with a finished project. I demonstrated the confidence, skills, and ability to complete the project as requested and in a timely fashion.

My perception of him as a leader changed after this project. What a shame, I thought so highly of him. My level of respect decreased.

> *"Wherefore, my beloved brethren, let every man be swift to hear, slow to speak, slow to wrath:"* (James 1: 19)

It wasn't necessary for him to repeat the instructions. I recorded them to be certain what was expected of me. I wanted to tell him. *"I heard you the first time."* I could only grin and bear it. He stereotyped me, placed a label on me, and I knew it. His behavior towards me revealed it.

Do It To Them Before They Do It To You

In the Hood the above saying is true. You don't let anybody get over on you so always stay one step ahead in the game. Stay on top of your game. A schoolmate of mine gave me this phrase *Do It To Them Before They Do It To You*, and showed me there's a difference in how the world operates and how God operates.

You see child of God, it's not good to steal or take from another and call it your own and the Word of God gives countless examples of this. King Ahab did this when he coveted the garden of another. He was in big trouble afterwards. (1 Kings 21) He misused his authority and suffered greatly for it.

My high school friend and I were talking when she spoke those words and it opened my eyes, I realized everyone doesn't operate under the principles of God. I soon learned that others will misuse you and think nothing of it. I wasn't serving God when she told me this, actually I had no relationship with him then. But I knew *"What goes around comes around,"* and I didn't want any bad things to happen to me. So I didn't try to manipulate or get over on anybody. I feared God that much.

Once salvation entered my life I realized where those sayings came from. I saw the value in allowing God's way to manifest itself rather than the worlds way. Now my friend's words are used for the Good when we use His way of getting results. The Golden Rule is appropriate.

> *"And as ye would that men should do to you, do ye also to them likewise."* (Luke 6: 31)

"Do unto others as you would have others do unto you" is what church people say. It means, however you want to be treated is the way you treat others. It's that simple. You love others the way you want to be loved. God

will judge you based on your actions, not on the actions of others. When we serve him with a pure heart he is well-pleased. I've seen him pour out blessings for following those principles. And I've seen people miss blessings for handling situations their own way. It's even happened to me a couple of times and I know better now.

A good leader knows a mutual respect must exist between individuals for the Good of everyone in the organization. It supersedes personal success. For the love of money, greed and exploitation has damaged so many people. With mutual respect comes the knowledge that when I treat you with respect you in turn will respect me in my position. A great leader takes it a step further. He knows that in order to lead he must understand and oftentimes walk in the shoes of those he is leading. He is leading as one who knows and has experienced the path of life his fellow workers are walking. He sets the example of behavior to exemplify when certain circumstances are encountered in this life with its many pains and many joys. He knows he is the head of the group, but not to emphasize lordship over another just because of position.

Now, a great leader is aware there's a value on the inside to impart that will cause fellow laborers to be better individuals and work for the common Good of all mankind. He knows the struggles he's endured will help others to overcome. By walking in those same shoes he won't step on you. He won't put out your fire because he recognizes that same fire in you and he won't extinguish it! That's what makes a good leader a great one. It may even cause him pain for a moment but he knows how to extract the best out of you. Just when you've reached your limits, the point of birthing greatness within you is ready, and he knows it's time to push you to your greatest potential and break forth the Good!

Do It To Them Before They Do It To You takes a brand new spin when you're pushing someone to greatness. Wow! Maybe my friends' words from the Hood can be used for the Good!

CONFIDENCE IN GOD

★ ★ ★

Put on the Whole Armor ✶ ✶ ✶

In the Hood you have to develop ways to protect yourself. You guard your heart and mind to prevent foreign objects from penetrating your protective covering. It's your way of saying you're in control and you allow nothing and no one to cross that line. Your guard shelters you from being hurt. Your shield implies, *I won't allow you to hurt me so I'll let you think you have advantage in one area to see how you play it out, but not really. It's an area I really care nothing about. "I" can handle it, but the real me you can't touch.*

God says NO! Let me handle it. Open yourself to me. Put away the knife, gun, and shield that you've invented for your own protection. Put away your unbelief. Put away your doubt. To believe me and trust me, means you have to take away your guard and put on my armor. You have to trust me and allow me to do as I said I would do. When you put down your guard you'll see that I've been there all along and you didn't need that old guard up anyway.

So stop telling yourself you can handle that lie you've invented for your own protection. It's never fully worked, it's prevented you from letting go and letting me heal that place of low self-esteem. You know it, that place that you've guarded so well, so long; that inner-most haven that you've created to shelter you from the storm. I'm in control of the storm. Did I not speak to it? Saying *"Peace be still?"* (St. Mark 4: 39) Did I not command the waves and the waters to obey me? Did I not change the atmosphere by my words? Let me in that guarded place and just believe me. You're already out there so far from shore anyhow. You've trusted me this far. You see what I can do when you're not thinking about it. You see how I take care of you beyond your own comprehension. You see the great joy and great peace that I bring when you trust me. Get rid of that Lie – you don't need it. I really am who I say I am. The Great I AM!

As we walk from day-to-day we need God's armor to protect us from the snares of the day. It is the ultimate protection.

"Be ye therefore followers of God, as dear children; And **walk in love**, *as Christ also hath loved us, and hath given himself for us an offering and a sacrifice to God for a sweetsmelling savour."* (Ephesians 5: 1, 2)

"Put on the whole armour of God, that ye may be able to stand against the wiles of the devil." (Ephesians 6: 11)

His armor is Love:
Loins girt about with truth
Breastplate of righteousness
Feet shod with the preparation of the gospel of peace
Shield of Faith
Helmet of Salvation
Sword of the Spirit
Praying always

Seal the Deal ✶ ✶ ✶

If you plan to succeed in business, observe the methods they use for conducting business where you are. If I were in Spain, I'd have to understand that culture, customs, and values. Americans are motivated by money, prestige, and favor. Hispanics are motivated by family values, and preservation of the family. Whereas Americans take an hour lunch to eat and to conduct business with a business transaction at the forefront of their agenda; Hispanics may take two hour lunches to eat a meal at home with a client and still may not resolve the business at hand. Their focus is building solid relations with one another before contracts are signed. Their business customs dictate a different set of priorities.

And any good business person knows - to gain the favor of a client, you honor their customs before any business is discussed. That's what wining and dining a client is all about.

We've been given instructions on how to conduct business in the book of Ruth. The book of Ruth is about a family who left their homeland during a famine. The mother, Naomi, loses her sons and her husband Elimelech, away from her homeland and returns with her daughter-in-law, Ruth.

Boaz was a kinsman of Naomi's husband, Elimelech. Boaz was also a mighty man of wealth who wanted Ruth, as his wife. She was a foreigner and the in-law of Naomi. With Naomi and Ruth's husbands both deceased, there were certain laws governing marriage and inheritances in Israel. Boaz followed these business customs to seal the deal for his bride. Following Naomi's instructions, Ruth also followed customs and affirmed her desire to marry Boaz.

According to their customs, the nearest male blood relative, known as the *kinsman redeemer*, was in position to marry Ruth if he was willing to redeem her. The requirements of a kinsman redeemer were three: Be in position as the nearest kin, be able to pay the price and make the purchase, and be willing to redeem. Boaz met two requirements, he could pay the price to redeem her with his wealth and he was willing to pay the price with his love for her, but he was not the nearest kinsman. Therefore, he needed to speak with the nearest of kin to negotiate a contract. Boaz observed these customs and conducted business accordingly. He immediately acted upon his love and faith.

First he waited at the gate. In that day, it was customary to conduct business transactions at the city gate. It was like a courthouse. In a courthouse you need witnesses to testify and validate the transaction. Boaz knew the kinsman was a businessman and would be there at some point during the day, so he waited for him at the city gate. Boaz was a savvy businessman himself; he was friendly and on good terms with the kinsman and with others in the community. He made arrangements to have every aspect of his plan in order. He brought witnesses to the business transaction at hand. Witnesses provided undisputed credibility. Whoever was conducting a business transaction asked their attendance for support.

Then, he presented the business proposition in full in the presence of these witnesses at the city gate. He was honest in his business dealings; he made no attempt to deceive the man. Boaz presented the kinsman's advantage first. The kinsman could redeem his right to Elimelech's property as the next in line, to which the kinsman agreed. Boaz proceeded to outline the entire responsibility of the redemption purchase which included marrying Ruth to comply with the law. This was a disadvantage to the kinsman; it would interfere with his own inheritance. Therefore, he could not purchase Elimelech's estate at this point. He declined the offer, then agreed to relinquish his position as the nearest male blood relative into the hand of Boaz, to which Boaz agreed.

Next, Boaz plucked off his shoe to seal the agreement and make the purchase. According to the custom, this plucking off of the shoe was his *Signature on the dotted line*, with onlookers as witnesses.

Finally he confirmed it before the elders. Now, it was legal for Boaz to marry Ruth and have rights to Elimelech's estate. The deal was sealed. Everyone was happy. Thus, Boaz completed the transaction whereby the inheritance was redeemed and Ruth became his wife. His approach was sincere and his method was approved before all. (Ruth 4 KJV)

In today's world our observance of other customs and business is conducted serves as a reminder that God does everything *"Decently and in order."* (1 Cor 14:40) He tells us to recognize and respect the powers that be.

> *"Let every soul be subject unto the higher powers. For there is no power but of God the powers that be are ordained of God. Whosoever therefore resisteth the power, resisteth the ordinance of God: and they that resist shall receive to themselves damnation."* (Romans 13: 1-2)

It's easier to complete a business transaction when you respect and honor others in their positions, customs, and ways of governing. Your respectability is noted quicker than one who commands their own agenda doing things their own way.

Go Ahead and Seal the Deal!

Thanks for the Promotion God! ✷ ✷ ✷

"For promotion cometh neither from the east, or from the west, nor from the south. But God is the judge: he putteth down one, and he setteth up another." (Psalms 75:6)

Elevate – To the Next Level
Experience – In God
Exposure - To Kings
Entry – The Open Door

Promotion comes from God. When you're not thinking about it – you're there. When your mind is far from it – He sets you before others. When service is your motive, then God shows up to utilize and capitalize on his investment – You! God is the biggest stock broker you'll ever meet. All the time you've invested in sin, he'll get a return on it. Every victory you've attained – he'll use it for his glory. His investments & stocks always give a 100% return. So you're never taking a chance when you step out on Him. It's a win-win sure deal!

Elevate - To the Next Level ✷ ✷ ✷

How do you elevate in God once you realize he has a mission and a plan for you? Going to the next level begins with prayer and the Word of God. Elevating in God has nothing to do with your will and your own motives. He elevates and transforms those who know him and who walk closely to him. Simply meaning you take him at his Word.

Remember Peter, James, and John? (If you don't, the story is in St. Mark 9) These men developed a relationship with Jesus. As they walked close to Jesus, he gave them a special revelation of him and he was transfigured right before their eyes. Transfigured means he changed his appearance. Now that's elevation of the highest kind.

Our greatest visualization today of a transfiguration is seen through the television set. In a matter of seconds we see a man change his normal appearance on television and it's enlightening. But it's second hand. Those lights, cameras, and effects are making it possible for you to visualize the change and it's not real. I can't imagine the lasting effect Jesus' transformation had on those disciples. They witnessed Jesus changing with their own eyes, a first hand account. He changed into an illuminating figure with white brightness all about him. Hey! Hey! The closer you walk with God, the higher up you go, and the more your eyes open.

These gentlemen obviously had a closer relationship than the other disciples. Perhaps they sacrificed a lot, were obedient, and were faithful. I don't know for sure but there had to be a difference. Elevation requires going to a higher dimension to achieve his will and as you begin to acquire the mind of Christ, you find yourself right with him in a solid spiritual place, seeking to please him no matter what it costs you. Your will is dead then, it's strictly his will. It happens when he's able to trust you. Jesus took them up on this mountain and transfigured himself before them. He trusted them not to mention what they saw on that mountain to any other man. He knew they were in a position to receive this elevation. When it's time God will make the move, you don't have to seek it, just seek him. And you'll be glad you did!

Experience-In God ✶ ✶ ✶

Your experience in the Word and your experiences with God in private, in prayer, and in action - allowing him to be God, will lead to your elevation. The more time you spend with him in prayer and in his Word the greater experiences you share. Faith comes by stepping beyond the ground you've already tread upon. Anytime God used an individual, he gave them an unforgettable experience. You're not required to walk with God 20 years for him to use you, but you do have to surrender and give him time to work his will in you and through you. He'll qualify you and use you in his kingdom for any position.

David became the King of Israel. Before that, he worked as a shepherd boy, he slew a lion and a bear, ran for his life from a jealous Saul, was despised and rejected and then…and then…and then… He became King of Israel.

Joseph was the Governor of Egypt and saved an entire nation of people by that position. But first he was hated of his brothers (his own blood brothers), sold into slavery and put into a pit, went to prison as a result of a lie told on him, then… he was made a governor in the palace. Experience – God tries you as gold is purified before he elevates you.

Moses was born to lead God's people out of bondage, and saved millions of souls. He was raised in the palace for 40 years to learn their customs. He murdered a man trying to defend one of his brethren and was on the run from the Pharaoh. He tended sheep for 40 years in a strange country and spent another 40 years learning how God wanted him to lead. And then …he faced that same Pharaoh he ran away from – but he had power when he saw him again.

All these men were elevated by their God-ordained experiences. They were the best of leaders. King David ruled an entire nation, Joseph saved an entire nation from destruction, Moses led millions to safety. By looking at the amount of people they ministered to and the lives they saved we see how God was glorified in each one of their lives. Their experiences prepared them for the greatest moves of God in history. But it was His Call. He gave the vision and the experience for his names sake.

Every experience was used for the Good.

Exposure-To Kings ✶ ✶ ✶

Can you imagine what Moses was thinking when God told him he was going back to Egypt to see Pharaoh again? I mean, the last time Moses heard about Pharaoh was when he left Egypt for murdering a man, Moses wasn't looking back! He was on the run for murder. *Now Jehovah, you're telling me to go back?* They had 'Wanted' posters up on the billboards for him. I imagine his thoughts were something like this, *"Will I be tried for murder, and will they stone me? Come on God Almighty, those Egyptians aren't playing and I can't face him. You've got to be kidding."*

Moses was a changed man after his encounter with God on the mountain. His experience visualizing a burning bush that did not burn up was a demonstration of God's miracle working power. He had specific instructions and by this time, Moses knew whom he trusted. Actually God Almighty uses our experiences to expose us to others to raise awareness of who he is. This key was his means to elect Moses for the job. And God said unto Moses, *"I AM THAT I AM."* (Exodus 3:14) Now Moses possessed the key to appearing before Pharaoh.

When Joseph (Genesis 45) was reunited with his brethren, he was a changed man! While in prison he interpreted dreams for the baker and the butler. When it came time for him to be exposed to others for the glory of God, he was ready. The Pharaoh in Egypt had a disturbing dream and needed his dream interpreted. The magicians and wise men of Egypt in his kingdom could not interpret the dream. They were no match for the God of Israel.

Joseph was an Israelite, who could interpret dreams, and who lived in a strange land now - Egypt. The Pharaoh of Egypt had a dream that needed interpretation. Since the dream came from God, Pharaoh needed a godly man, one of God's own servants to interpret it. Unless you're connected to God you cannot discern spiritual things. *"But the natural man receiveth not he things of the Spirit of God: for they are foolishness unto him: neither can he know them because they are spiritually discerned."* (1 Corn. 2:14) Thus, Joseph's gift was exposed to someone with authority and power to open a door of opportunity for him.

The need arose for a governor in Egypt and the demonstration of godly character by Joseph interpreting the Pharaoh's dream promoted God's agenda to save his people. Although Joseph was in a foreign environment it did not change who he was. Joseph's exposure set him in a position to save lives.

David (1 Samuel 17) experienced a similar exposure. He was instructed to check on his brothers at war. His prior experience with a lion and a bear made him unafraid of a nine foot giant, Goliath. Once he slew that giant he won the kings daughter and it placed him in position for kingship.

These are examples of God exposing faithful servants to powerful leaders of their day. Their experiences were phenomenal and not everyday occurrences once God's powerful touch intervened.

All the years you spend preaching, teaching, witnessing, cleaning, administrating, singing, praying, reading, fasting, serving others, loving, sacrificing, and just serving God will give you exposure to others. No matter how minute or small, he'll use it for his glory.

I've visited a few churches, gone to a few singings, and been faithful in service because I loved God. Now I see it differently than before. All the people I've had fellowship with remember me and recognize the God in me. Although I was in attendance at many events, I didn't think much attention was given me being a woman of few words. What seems insignificant one day may be significant later on. Just be faithful to God. Not to be seen or heard. **Love Him!**

Entry – The Open Door ✷ ✷ ✷

Me a Television Show Host!?!?

LOL Laughing out Loud! God has a sense of Humor! In my wildest dreams I could not have, would not have, dare not say, that I would be a television show hostess. Say it isn't so? I still pinch myself to see if I'm dreaming.

Please check it out. God called me to the ministry. So, I determined I'd be the best minister I could be since I had no choice in *that* matter. My purse was small, that means I had very little money, and because of my humble beginnings in a little old sanctified church, I did not think about seminary or attending a big school to be trained for ministry. I prayed and fasted much, looked around at the resources available and went to work. I taught Sunday school for many years and loved it, but my audience was limited to my own church. I didn't venture outside those walls, except to visit other churches when we fellowshipped or at a singing event. Even then, I just gave my testimony. Therefore, I decided to prepare myself to minister to the world.

Prepare. Prepare. Prepare. Johnny Cochran said these words as the keynote speaker for a Central State University graduation I attended…Prepare to *speak and minister to the world Sherry* were the sentiments of my mind and heart. *Don't limit yourself to these four walls.* Although I stood before the congregation every Sunday with my Sunday School class, I still lacked sophisticated speaking skills that would require me to stand before larger audiences.

I desired to engage in conversations with every person I meet, not only on a platform, but on a personal level too. I love sharing Jesus! (He's so good) And, you can't be limited to your own way of thinking when sharing his goodness. The best preacher prepares him/herself to stand before the world to preach this wonderful gospel in every possible way, whether on the street corner or in the white house. God had given me specific instructions about being not just a minister, but a preacher. So I needed and wanted to be well-versed in current events; I desired the best training possible.

I was already well-versed in the scriptures. Teaching Sunday school kept me sharp in the Word. Our superintendent believed you had to be the best. Therefore, as a lower level class instructor (I taught the best age 6-8), he demanded us to stay current with the adult Sunday School lesson as well as our own lesson. Teaching lower level helps you relate to the basic understanding level of learning and minister to all souls. We had a unique blend.

I desired to walk into a room and talk to people without getting nervous. I'm the type of person who needs a classroom setting and interaction with others to get the most out of me, so I joined Toastmasters.

Boy what a move! This was a great step to take in overcoming my insecurities. I loved the table topics, the two-minute speeches that prompted you to give an answer on current events with no foreknowledge of the topic in questions. It prompted you to keep current on news. You had no idea what would be asked. This type of interaction sharpens you.

After working with Toastmasters for a few months, I was nominated to enter a speech contest. My friend Teresa decided to video tape the contest for me. I did not realize the impact it would have. I did well. The video was aired on the community access channel and that was the beginning of something great. People told me they saw it – I was amazed and surprised, people saw me on television.

Not only that, but this was a door opening up for me as a result of me stepping out to fulfill the mission God set before me (although I didn't know what it was). God doesn't always tell you everything, he lets you find your way…He gives you just enough information to motivate you to action.

During this venture I met Dr. Janet Climmons. We hit it off right away and she interviewed me for her program, "Standing on the Promises." We did two interviews and we talked about ministry. She shared her plans to leave Langston for a period and wanted me as her guest host until she returned. I could not believe it, me, hosting a program on television? Imagine that? I wasn't sure she was serious but I was honored to be asked and I knew *it had* to be God. What's funny is that God had shown it to me a couple years prior but I had no understanding of the dream at the time. I even spoke it to my pastor by telling him I was going to be on television one day. I had no idea what I was speaking. The words just came from my mouth prophetically.

We don't always understand what God is doing, but we know he's up to something Great!

Transitioning: From The HOOD To The GOOD

Mistaken Identity - I'm Gonna Be Me!

It's a mistake to judge another individual by the way they look. Just because you're a tall dark male, doesn't mean you're a threat to someone. Unfortunately that's a stereotype that men live with. Or, because you're a light skinned female doesn't mean that you are conceited. Or, because you're blond doesn't mean you dumb. Some people have been told certain things about outward features you have and treat you accordingly, but it should not make you react to their ill-treatment of you.

The God within me refuses to allow another human being to influence me to become what God never intended. I've seen people do things to try and upset me when I know I'm bigger than that. They were mistaken. I don't react violently to everything or when things don't go my way. I've not allowed that to characterize me. The more someone tries to provoke me, the closer I get to Jesus because he's the one I look to.

I've had co-workers throw and project negative situations my way to influence a violent or loud reaction only to be disappointed! I refuse to bow down to their level. I can count on one hand how many fights I've been in throughout my life and how many people I've engaged in an argument with. Sorry folks but I refuse to operate like that. I made choices a long time ago to let God direct my footsteps and I'm not going to let anyone provoke me in any way.

In a work environment, professional conduct is always acceptable. Any other conduct is unacceptable because the purpose for being in the work place is to conduct business and earn a living. It is always in order to be cordial and maintain a professional demeanor when in the workplace and also in public.

I had to learn that sometimes people expect certain behavior from you because of how you look without ever knowing anything about your character. This was alarming to me, but a lesson well-learned. Just because I've been stereotyped does not require me to comply. I am going to be me, I rather enjoy being myself. It's easier than being *the somebody else* I'm expected to be!

A Servant of the Most High God

In my early years, I spent a lot of my time witnessing to others and sharing His goodness wherever I'd go. At lunch time I'd go to the courthouse square and since I loved meeting people, it was an opportunity to share the gospel over lunch. On my trip to and from work, I met many people on the bus. I just love sharing Jesus, his love, his power. By nature I've always been quiet but once God saved me the boldness to share his message with others began to increase within me. This didn't happen overnight though. Many times I was afraid to speak up because I just didn't talk to people like that. I was quiet so a lot of work had to take place for me to share.

Very often I used Gideon's method of making sure God was speaking to me. He put a fleece (a piece of wool) out before God and asked God to make it wet all around the fleece as a sign he was hearing the voice of God. Sometimes we need a sign to know he's speaking. I did this countless times when I did not have the nerve to talk to people. I was very nervous and afraid. One time I was on the bus and there was an older gentleman sitting along the side seat in front of me. God said *"Tell him Jesus Loves You."* Of course I was scared. Maybe he'd think I was crazy or something, I don't know. But I told God *"You have to let me know this is you talking some kind of way."* Next thing I know the man was staring straight at me (right down my throat). So I had to speak up. My fears were calmed afterwards because the man favorably received me.

Another time a young girl's baby was crying and turning red. I felt the need to pray as I sat there reading my bible. I was afraid of rejection so I was scared she would say no. To my surprise, (once I finally got the nerve to speak up) she was glad to let me pray for her child. The baby calmed down immediately and stopped crying. God was at work! I think some of those times I was afraid God might decide not to move this moment, or maybe my prayer wouldn't take affect and I'd be embarrassed. Funny thing is, the more I stepped out on his Word, the more confidence I gained in him working through me.

One day, after many years of witnessing to others on that bus, in the neighborhood, and many other places, God gave me a format to share his good news. **Walking In Victory (WIV).** WIV is a talk program where I've interviewed people in the community to share the great news of the gospel. I have met so many wonderful people. It has blessed *me* more than the listening audience. I am overjoyed at the work God is doing on the program.

I meet people throughout the city and get very positive feedback. It's wonderful to witness God working in the lives of his people. I am blessed that he has chosen me for such a task.

God's way of blessing exceeds ours. He knows what we love to do and the effectiveness we'll have in working for Him.

The Unwritten Rules

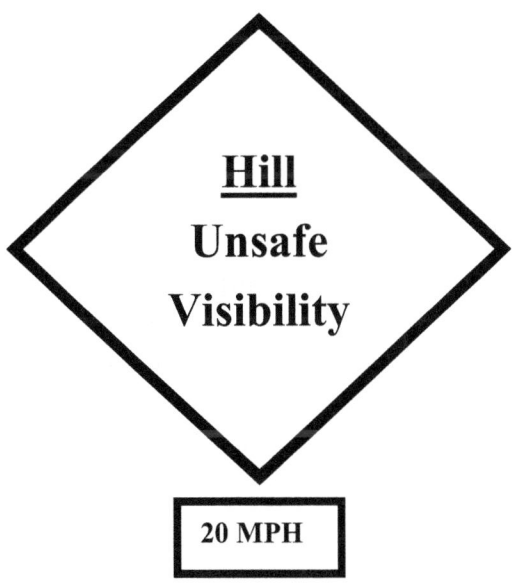

Every culture, community, race has unwritten rules they govern themselves by. The sign above is a written rule I looked upon in my travels one day in my neighborhood. It should have encouraged me to slow down to avoid a collision of any sort.

I took notice of it strangely, it caused me to think about my actions. I can't recall seeing the sign before and it really surprised me. I'd never noticed a sign like that in my many years of driving in the city. And I've been on many streets. I've been on this street many times before this particular day.

From the Hood to the Good — Sherry Styles

In the Hood, you do what it takes to survive. You're governed by your own set of rules. I really wasn't attempting to go the speed limit because I had my own mind when I turned on that street. I was in a hurry going somewhere. (that's always) That's the unwritten rule, you have your own set of rules. Forget the signs - it's my way or no way. So I'll cut across or go as fast as I want.

There used to be a time in my city, when you rode through the suburbs, you drove the speed limit. You know the rules – they don't play. You will get a ticket! Everybody slows down to the speed limit there.

When I saw this sign it motivated me to think about slowing down and I did. How many times do the unwritten rules govern us and get us into trouble? Rules are in place for a reason and usually it's for our own protection. It keeps us in line and safe when we follow them. Can you imagine a world where there were no rules or laws to govern us and everyone did their own thing, followed their own mind? What chaos would exist! I don't think the world would exist very long. The wrong values would emerge and no one would get along for very long (five minutes).

My unwritten rule did not work on this street. I discarded my notion of doing what I wanted immediately. Safety was an issue. I've heard that familiarity breeds disrespect. We can become so familiar with our way of existing and doing things that we fail to recognize something valuable. Why do Christians stay in the Word? It's too easy to veer off track. Sometimes the unwritten rules are no good in the Hood, or the suburbs, or wherever you are. Every neighborhood and every culture has them.

Unwritten rules should be cast aside when Truth is revealed. Truth can take you to heights you never imagined. Truth can also save your life.

A hill makes visibility difficult in a residential area. Children play, people walk, dogs roam. It's a time to decrease speed and slow down to acknowledge the innocent ones. The little ones that don't have the perception you've acquired yet. There are little ones who may wander in the wrong path and need your alert driving skills to keep the neighborhood safe.

That day I slowed down and took notice of the neighborhood in a slightly different way. God sure has a way of getting your attention. I'm certainly glad he did. My unwritten rule could be dangerous to everyone, especially when a written rule is present to deter my thinking.

Perhaps our Unwritten rules need evaluation.

Have A Little Respect – I'm A Professional

My pressed and curl days are over. That ended when I started high school. I don't have to do my own relaxers anymore either; especially when hair stylists give you the professional look for a few dollars more. So why do I revert back to my old ways when times get tough? I'm used to surviving the best way I can and can't help doing what I know to make it. I'm learning that trusting God is not an option even when money is tight. I must do so (trust Him) in order to stand in this day and time.

I did not have all of my rent money and was trying to save the little I had to pay my rent. Well, my hair needs to be done and I need the professional look, it lasts longer. It's a tight spot to be in that mandates prayer for a solution. So I nixed having my niece do my hair for a few dollars and off the beauty shop I go for the professional look. I decided to trust God for my rent. I stepped out on faith to *see what happens!*

The results are always better to trust God. The truth is, God wants you to feel good about yourself, to exemplify confidence and to have a little dignity about yourself. Don't walk in places with your hands extended unless it's to be a blessing. I couldn't tell my beautician I didn't have the money, but I could tell God. My beautician is a professional and the service she gives is outstanding. Every woman who leaves her chair is beautiful when she leaves. It's also true she's a great stylist. Be glad someone can give you professional service and be willing to pay them for it. When you accept less than the best you will lose in the end. Pay the full amount now and later you won't have to pay again or have to do it over.

Blessings are flowing. You may be holding on to something that will ultimately bless you. Release it. It's in your destiny to be blessed as God's child. Timing is everything when releasing. Don't be stingy or cheap – Give it up!

Relax & Wear Your Jeans

Jeans represent cute & comfortable to me. The corporate world has taken the notion in the last 15 years to be casual on Friday, saying it's okay to wear jeans as a way to relieve stress in the workplace.

For so long I've been in highly stressed positions. We allow our work situations and home life to stress us and sometimes without realizing the impact these things are having on us mentally, physically, and emotionally. Spiritual balance helps to overcome imbalance in these areas.

I was working for a company and it was jeans day. A co-worker and I were discussing wearing jeans and I imparted to her my difficulty in making the transition from professional attire to jeans.

In previous days jeans were unacceptable in the workplace. As an HR representative at a corporation, professional attire was the norm, i.e. suit or jacket, skirt & blouse, dress pants & shirt with a tie. There were times when we could "dress down." It was called "country club causal." That meant nothing less than kakis and a polo shirt for guys and nice slacks/skirt with a nice blouse for women. I was trained for this. I prepared myself to move up in the company by taking classes and they taught you to "Dress for Success." The goal was to project the image of your future job or position by dressing the part, thereby, alerting upper management to the seriousness of your intentions and also to engrain in your mind the place you're going to. After a while you start to believe it yourself and the image is projected in all you do. This worked well with me because it changed my mindset. It also improved my rapport with my co-workers and those who are looking at prospective employees for their department. I left a good professional impression.

From the Hood to the Good — Sherry Styles

I like being comfortable, no frills for me! So it took a while for me to learn to "dress the part." Although I like to dress nicely, I always have to think twice before I leave home. Where I'm going, who'll be there, and what the event is. (I already know who I am) But everybody wants to fit in without being too far out don't they? Well maybe not, cause some don't care. Some try to make a statement by being different and that's okay. I have to think about who *I* am and the perception of me when I step out the door. And just being comfortable relaxes my mind a little too much, especially wearing jeans. It takes me way back in time. After all it is a privilege.

So here I am trying to make the transition. The work place carries a certain respect. It is a place of business. Not for play clothes. It is not your personal place, therefore you dress appropriately so as not to entice, disrespect, or distract others who have a job too. Making this transition was difficult because of my "Dress for Success" training. The spiritual transition I made also affected my image. My life changed once God stepped into my life, and not only did the inner woman change, but my apparel and image changed right along with the internal change. So wearing jeans to work is not easy.

Jeans represent being yourself and comfortable. Relaxation and comfort also come to mind. Throw in less stress, friendship, and lastly *style*. You can tell a lot about people by the jeans they wear and the event they're wearing them to. I say relax and put on your jeans but still look cute!

Well, I did wear jeans that day because I didn't want to be a party pooper. I wore them starched, with a pair of yellow/gold heels, yellow/gold top and a gold blazer to match. It took a lot for me to do it. But I relaxed and wore my jeans and felt good about it.

Move to the Head of the Class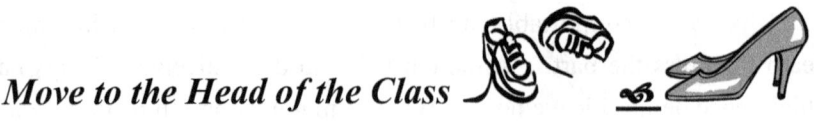

Its time to move to the Head of the Class. Stop focusing on your lack. People with low self-esteem sit in the back of a room to hide. Afraid to make a mistake, afraid they're alone in their thinking. They're hiding.

Quiz: See if you have the Hood Mentality or if you're developing the Good Mentality.

You are on the job and the boss asks everyone a question. You have a great idea for the solution and you know it. Because you've shown great potential in the past, your co-workers kind of hem-haw around waiting on you to speak. You share your idea. They all reword your idea and give credit to your boss. How do you handle this?

1 – Take it in stride and ignore, that's just how they are
2 – Call them on it by telling them about themselves
3 – Reword it, so you still get the credit

In every culture there is a hierarchy, an order of doing things. Each level is established with a determined function at that level. Initiating an action outside of the hierarchy can get you nowhere in most cultures. Your actions aren't even recognized until you contact the appropriate person in command. It's just a matter of respect given to the office.

Since our creator established a method and way of conducting business, he's the first provide an example to follow. Even when King Ahab was wrong, God did not address the people in the kingdom for his misbehavior. God went directly to him. You must access yourself to the person at each level to gain attention. When you respect the proper authority, that respect is in turn granted to you.

In the example above you'll receive the accolades for it if you take it in stride and ignore their strategy, #1. The truth is, they know you initiated the idea from the beginning and obviously you are a good source of creativity and innovation. That's why they want to use it!

No more hiding, no more Fear – Move!

I'm On The Clock

It is fun to have a computer with the latest and the greatest gadgets and software. It sure is fun to play around with this technology and learn how it functions when it's right there on your desk at your fingertips whenever you want. Computers are fascinating. Today's technology gives you games, creative software and so much more. And once you have a few moments to spare investigating its functionality, those moments turn into hours. But NOT ON COMPANY TIME!

You were not hired to fool around with the software. A strong work ethic implies that you have standards in your conduct. Don't cheat your employer. No matter how alluring or intriguing the computer is – use it on your OWN PERSONAL TIME: Lunchtime, before your scheduled work time, or after work and **only if your boss permits it**. There's a time and a place for all things. (Ecclesiastes 3:1) Work is not the place for personal use of office facilities. Please use *your time* to search the web, preferably at another place.

"And he said unto them, Render therefore unto Caesar the things which h be Caesar's, and unto God the things which be God's." (Luke 20: 25)

Walking

In The

GOOD

Walking in the Good

You have the Victory! Keep saying this over and over and over because you need to repeat it daily. Reinforce it in your mind. Your environment has negatives all round that reinforce otherwise. These statements are reinforced daily:

> You will fail
> No use in trying that
> You tried before and it didn't work
> Nobody's going to pay attention to you
> That's just stupid
> Don't try that
> Nobody's going to hear that
> You must be crazy
> You're a failure
> You can't do that

I could go on. I know at least three of those messages have stopped you in your track from pursuing an idea you had. It's embedded in your psyche and shows up when you least expect. But I discovered something about that. If it's not a good idea you can only find out once you pursue it. If it's a good idea you can only find out once you pursue it. If it's a God idea you can only find out once you pursue it. You must try and exhaust every phase of your idea until you're convinced. Pursue your ideas.

When you consult your sources you'll know whether you can walk through a path. If it's designated for your success – consulting God will reveal whether or not to enter therein. If not, you'll rid yourself of it ebbing away at your mind and you can close the book on it.

Suppose we take a victorious attitude and alter the messages above:

> I will fail if I don' try
> I can't fail, because I'll learn something just by trying
> I better at least try it
> Try it this time, I forgot something last time, it'll work this time
> Somebody will pay attention to me
> That's just brilliant
> Try that, somebody's going to hear that
> I'll be crazy if I don't
> I must be crazy to listen to others
> I'm a success, I'm a winner
> *I can do all things through Christ who strengthens me*
> If God be for me who can be against me

You see, now counteract those negatives by feeding your mind with the right food. Success breads success. Peace casts away anger. Love casts out fear. Joy removes discouragement. Get the picture. You have the victory don't let anyone steal it from you.

Having a right attitude is 90% of the battle according to Charles Swindol[3]. And he's right! Once you recognize you are a joint-heir with Christ, you won't permit wrong influences to dominate your thinking, your time, or your resources. Total focus on Christ will push everything else out of focus and you'll devote full concentration to your mission.

Distractions are designed to zap our focus, our energy, and our time. Discouragement sets in soon afterwards and a disheartening follows with this message, *"What's the use it's not going to be fulfilled."* Truly, truly I know

---

[3] "Attitude"

you've felt this way and half-heartedly go about your mission with this type of thinking in your head.

When you trace back your thoughts you can pinpoint the hour, the person, the exact words (spirit), and the thoughts afterwards that distracted your attention away from your goal. It is like a downward spiral. Once you accept the first negative, all the others are waiting their turn to take you down…down…down to the pit.

Let's just reverse that downward spiral and issue a whirlwind upward. Counteract that negative with a positive, look up to heaven, and think on good things. It's your choice! You'll be energized and your strength remains to move forward in your designated purpose. Up! Up! Up! and Away! to the heavens where God is waiting for you to snap back and remember that you're his child. You have the victory no matter how you look at it. Things go better with Christ on your side.

Hear me and hear me good. Don't get mad or angry with the person who has a negative spirit. They may not recognize what's happening. As long as you recognize what's happening you control the outcome. God is in control! And that gives you the right to praise him at any time to move darkness away from you. You have the victory!

As you transition from the Hood to the Good your entire attitude moves to knowing who you are and walking in your ordained purpose.

Don't Stop Dreaming

Have you ever had a dream and you saw yourself in a great place and couldn't believe it was you? Did you wonder how you got there? If so, my advice to you is - Don't stop dreaming. It is when you stop dreaming that you fall into the world's way of living. The hustle and bustle to go here, and there to survive is the world's way of living. Without having a passion to ignite your fire you miss the peace of God. God gives dreams to let you know the snares of life have no hold on you. I know by my own experiences. In prayer, God took me to a special place where I knew he loved me. He gives you those moments in time to let you know it's going to be okay.

I was a young lady from the Hood when I had a dream. In the dream I saw greatness and I knew it was something I wanted. I held on to my dream. God told me the dream would be fulfilled and that it came from him.

Life is Good! Because of knowing Him! Breathtaking! The writer said Magnificent! The Power, Peace, and Presence of God makes you fall down and worship him. When he speaks, everything on earth pays attention and acknowledges his voice.

"The spirit of God hath made me, and the breath of the Almighty hath given me life." (Job 33: 4)

Dreams motivate us to live! Don't stop dreaming.

"Where there is not vision, the people perish"
Proverbs 29: 18

Awaken

Have you ever been asleep and did not know it? I read somewhere that we have to revisit those things that make us smile as children and we revive our souls. Life's complications take away us performing those simple things to awaken our abilities to be our very best. I gave to someone in need today and it felt good. It awakened that inner child.

What makes you thrive?! It's time to awaken your passions. We all have interests and passions that get our juices flowing. For some it is seeing their ideas come alive. For others, it's knowing they made a difference in someone's life. Stand without fear of being knocked down. You can't fear being knocked down. You must stand up for what you believe in – anyhow! Standing means in the face of ridicule, shame, and humiliation you are convinced in your belief strong enough to withstand the opposition.

Awaken to your destiny, it was given to you by someone who will help you perform it. Awaken! Now!

Show 'em Your Stuff

You're blessed! Let's establish that first. When you endeavor to walk with the Master, he blesses your pathway because you belong to him. Times come when we have to stand the test and our faith is under trial. Those times reveal to us how strong we are and where we need improvements. Standing a test requires preparation even when you don't realize the test is coming. Every tool and instrument for Victory is ordered before the test is presented to us in our daily walk. As we read the Word and pray we find God's testing of us is always a way to bless us.

The prophet Elijah faced such a dilemma when he challenged the prophets of Baal to a match. Their god against God Almighty! (Sounds uneven to me from the start) Nevertheless, the prophets of Baal believed in the god they worshipped so they accepted the duo and were not afraid of the challenge.

> *"And call ye on the name of your gods, and I will call on the name of the LORD: and the God that answereth by fire, let him be God. And all the people answered and said, it is well-spoken."* (I Kings 18: 24)

Order in the House

Elijah placed everything in proper order when he challenged the 450 prophets of Baal. Elijah knew a method for his God to respond. He knew God would not fail. He also knew to meet those prophets on terms they could understand and accept with a goal in mind. He knew the mind of his enemy, the false prophets, and he knew the mind of his God. And because he was sent by God and moved only at God's word, he was confident.

"And it came to pass after many days, that the word of the LORD came to Elijah in the third year, saying, Go, shew thyself unto Ahab; and I will send rain upon the earth." (I Kings 18: 1)

A person who refuses to have order in their life misses a great part of God for he does everything decently and in order. Chaos doesn't exist with him.

Drama = Chaos ≠ God

He loves order and is pleased when we represent his name that way. (1Cor. 14: 40) Whatever you endeavor to do, dot every i, cross every *t*, give no reason for ill reproach on yourself and you'll be glad you did.

ORDER = PEACE = God

There is nothing greater than an employee whose work area is neatly organized, clean, tidy, well decorated, and in order. Every time I've had a work review I noticed this area was on the review form to be evaluated. For me, maintaining a neat work area is just a part of me. I don't like dust and dirt, I just like being organized. It's sort of like an inspection. If your supervisor doesn't tell you to clean up your area when corporate comes around for the yearly visit, you're in good shape. If your supervisor has to speak to you about it, then put it on your to do list at least once per week.

"The steps of a good man are ordered by the LORD: and he delighteth in his way." (Psalms 37: 23)

Opposition and My Pet Peeve

Opposition and adversity face us on a daily basis as Christians but there's no reason for alarm. I think the days of innocence leave us quickly and a daily fight exists for survival in this world. The key to all this is to know is who is fighting with you and for you. We can't know total peace except we know God. And total peace is realized through adversity and opposition.

To know Jesus is to experience peace and love. The flip side of that coin is adversity. Just when I claim a right to his promises and exercise my right to be free in him, I open myself to opposition. I rejoice! I don't have to fight the battle anymore. I've come to realize I can't fight the battle alone. It's his job to fight them. So when opposition comes, I don't have to stop marching. It's then time for God's power to reign supreme in my life.

A pet peeve of mine is for and about young people. It deals with opposition and adversity. When trouble comes knocking at your door, the best way to avoid it is being involved in fulfilling your goals. You won't entertain foolishness when you have a goal to complete. And once you focus your attention on your goal the enemy comes to distract your attention away from fulfilling it. Strong forces intend to deceive you into thinking your belief in God is vain. That's when you know you're on to something great!

Let's get this straight. We know the *"devil is as a roaring lion seeking whom he may devour."* (1 Peter 5:8) He wants to take the best from you to devour you. God wants the best of you too for his glory. I've seen so many young men get into trouble because someone else influenced them to do something foolish. That foolish behavior took their best and most productive years by placing them in jail or causing them to have big time guilt for something they later regret. Anytime you're on the wrong path, God will talk to you personally to make changes; just as he has spoken to you personally to fulfill a vision. Don't abandon his vision. Take his way out although it may seem strange.

People who are busy working towards a goal, fulfilling a dream, or building a vision, don't have time to entertain foolishness. They say No! right away. Alternatively, those without a dream entertain foolishness because they have nothing better to do. I think they're waiting on the right influence to push them in the right direction. The key is to find something to do. Find something you're passionate about and enjoy. We live in the land of opportunity. There are many programs to educate you, help get you on your feet, point you in the right direction, and get you away from negative influences who are doing nothing and have no direction to follow. Take advantage of what's available to you.

The devil knows you have the potential to own something, become an outstanding entrepreneur, or even win a gold medal, so he'll send somebody who fell for his game to entice you. His game goes something like this:

Brother #1: Hey man, I don't have cash you got any?
Brother #2: No man.
Brother #1: Hey let's go rob a bank?
Brother#2: Well man, maybe. (Thinks for a minute or two has nothing better to do) Yeah man!

<u>OR:</u>

Brother #1: Hey man, I don't have cash you got any?
Brother #2: No man, but I'm going to school. I'll earn some.
Brother #1: Man that's jacked, I need money now! Hey let's go rob a bank?
Brother#2: Man, I'm going to school, cause I'm going to own a bank. Later for that!

The Hood will take your manhood away from you when you think you're gaining it. I can remember so many times that I witnessed to guys my brother and I grew up with and encouraged them to come to church. Many of them were just getting off the bus coming home from prison and they saw me first. I always had a gospel message. I know that works. God strategically placed me in their path to save their lives. With sadness I share with you that 100% of them tell me they wish they'd listened to me. They went right back to their old lifestyle, same friends who weren't trying to achieve anything positive. God knew and I knew their way out was Jesus Christ! Why lose your life to the street when you don't have to?

A man is at his best when he's providing for his family and has their respect as a result of being a husband, father, friend, and a provider. A system that can remove him from this position takes away his manhood.

My pet peeve is all about positioning and having a direction in your life; about keeping yourself on the right track. It takes a determination to stay on a good path. Honestly, I had no idea what career path to take. But when God changed my life, he gave me one. I used my interests for the kingdom of God. I developed them by educating myself and gaining knowledge.

I worked at a financial institution early in life, but was unsure of what direction to take. I prayed and asked God what to do. A brother at church and I were talking one day shortly afterwards, and he said to me, as long as he was in business, he was employed. I sought the counsel of God and it worked. I stayed in business and remained employed.

Staying connected to God has many advantages and I'm glad I sought his counsel and listened.

Opposition and Elijah

Every person alive faces opposition at least once in life. Even though the prophet Elijah spoke as the mouthpiece of God, he faced opposition. King Ahab was a king gone bad. He built an altar for an idol god Baal. (I Kings 16:30-33) Ahab's ways displeased God, so God sent Elijah to settle the score. God had to get the influence of Baal away from his people, just as he does with you. He tries to get negative influences away for your good, let him do it. At times others will blame God for their troubles when the fault is in them, as King Ahab did.

> *"And it came to pass, when Ahab saw Elijah, that Ahab said unto him, Art thou he that troubleth Israel? And he answered, I have not troubled Israel; but thou, and thy father's house, in that ye have forsaken the commandments of the LORD, and thou hast followed Baalim."* (1 Kings 18: 17,18)

Ahab was moving under the wrong influence and that bad influence was destined for destruction. Worship to any one or any entity other than the true and living God is false worship.

Elijah, a prophet of God, challenged them, the prophets of Baal, to this duo on Mt. Carmel, confidently fulfilling God's instructions. (I Kings 18: 24) Their god, Baal, could not and did not answer in this duo. (vs.26-29) Remember now, Ahab was a king over Israel so he influenced people by his position. Kings controlled the synagogues and ruled the land. Leaders influence us greatly, and every leader has a responsibility to maintain God as supreme.

A false god, a manmade god, or image cannot match God Almighty. His nature opposes the very character of God. The Baal worshippers began to cut themselves, that's not God's way. God Almighty wants you to love yourself and his word proves it over and over again. You don't have to oppose or hurt yourself. God is Love and he Loves you! His love is no match for a false sense of Love.

Old Testament *"Hear, O Israel: The LORD our God is one LORD: And thou shalt love the LORD thy God with all thine heart, and with all thy soul, and with all thy might."* (Deut. 6: 4-5)

New Testament *"Jesus said unto him, Thou shalt love the Lord thy God with all thy heart, and with all thy soul, and with all thy mind. This is the first and great commandment. And the second is like unto it, Thou shalt love thy neighbour as thyself."* (Matthew 22:37-39)

Outstanding Performance

"Let your light so shine before men, that they may see your good works, and glorify your Father which is in heaven." (Matthew 5:16)

Your light was meant to shine. I have worked for only a few company's in my lifetime, by being a faithful worker whom they wanted to employ. And they kept me around for a while. I made an effort to give outstanding performance to the best of my ability. I attended school to enhance my performance, and made a good show of my talents.

This same diligence is required of the person who sells drugs or tells a lie to deceive. (They often get away with it!) It's the constant and earnest effort to accomplish what is undertaken with persistent exertion of the body or mind. I often say that Hollywood doesn't have the best actors they exist right in your neighborhood. The diligence used to perform the negative transfers to the Good.

I observe people with "fast" money and their zest for living. I pray for them because when it's their time to serve God with their all, they will spare no expense for the kingdom. They excel at being the Best and having the best. They already possess that spirit of excellence that God is searching for in drawing others and giving outstanding performance. God wants to employ them, they're faithful at their job, precise in executing a task, seek the best to enhance their performance, and produce results. Outstanding performers. I've encountered people able to sell you your own house, very cunning and crafty. They understand people and what motivates individuals. Winning others with the truth requires the ability to understand people and motivating them to action. If I had Oscars I'd hand them out to those outstanding performers. I know quite a few. I meet them everyday. On the brink of an encounter with the savior, they are waiting on their chance to be seen and heard. It's in their nature to seek the Good to spring forth in their life. I was once there and now I want to see it come forth in someone else!

Now Elijah was determined to give outstanding performance. His challenge was based on an intelligent question:

> *"And Elijah came unto all the people, and said, **How long halt ye between two opinions?** if the LORD be God, follow him: but if Baal, then follow him. And the people answered him not a word."*
> (1Kings 18: 21)

Such a bold declaration is God's time to show up. He won't fail to show that he is God especially since he initiates the challenge. After the prophets of Baal agreed to the challenge, Elijah, a perfect gentleman, allowed them to go first.

> *"And Elijah said unto the prophets of Baal, Choose you one bullock for yourselves, and dress it first; for ye are many; and call on the name of your gods, but put no fire under. And they took the bullock which was given them, and they dressed it, and called on the name of Baal from morning even until noon, saying, O Baal, hear us. But there was no voice, nor any that answered. And they leaped upon the altar which was made."* (1 Kings 18:25, 26)

It's interesting to note the ability of their god. No answer, no voice, nothing. They began to get beside themselves. Here was a chance for their god to show his stuff, and he was nowhere to be found. Elijah thought it was funny. Four-hundred fifty (450) prophets following a god who can't produce results and here is one (1) standing, opposing so many. He mocked them:

> *"And it came to pass at noon, that Elijah mocked them, and said, Cry aloud: for he is a god; either he is talking, or he is pursuing, or he is in a journey, or peradventure he sleepeth, and must be awaked. And it came to pass, when midday was past, and they prophesied until the time of the offering of the evening sacrifice, that there was neither voice, nor any to answer, nor any that regarded."* (1 Kings 18:27, 29)

Elijah's experiences with God up to this point always produced results. (1 Kings 17: 14, 15, 21, 22, 24) After witnessing the no effects performance of Baal, Elijah asked the people to come near him. He remembered the heritage by which his faith was established in the God of Israel.

> *"And Elijah took twelve stones, according to the number of the tribes of the sons of Jacob, unto whom the word of the LORD came, saying, Israel shall be thy name"* (1 Kings 18: 31)

He rebuilt the altar they'd broken down with those twelve stones. He put everything in order and commanded four barrels of water be poured over the sacrifice three times. Now remember his challenge, *"the God that answereth by fire, let him be God."* Water drenched the altar and filled the trenches. It was evening sacrifice time now and Elijah's turn to call upon his God.

> *"Elijah the prophet came near, and said, LORD God of Abraham, Isaac, and of Israel, let it be known this day that thou art God in Israel, and that I am thy servant, and that I have done all these things at thy word.*

Hear me, O LORD, hear me, that this people may know that thou art the LORD God, and that thou hast turned their heart back again. **Then the fire of the LORD fell,** *and consumed the burnt sacrifice, and the wood, and the stones, and the dust, and licked up the water that was in the trench."* (1 Kings 18: 36-38)

God did it. He even gave them an opportunity to get it right. *(that thou hast turned their heart back again)* Outstanding performance! God will show up! God's performances are a demonstration of his love to capture their hearts in service to him. Why serve a god that cannot work for you? Perhaps they were deceived into thinking the use of incantations, spells, divination, and manipulations were powerful enough to win in this life. The results here indicate they only cause harm in the end. God's love protects, covers, and keeps you. God showed up and showed out with Love! He always, always, always gives us a chance to get it right. He loves you just that much. Thank God for Grace.

Overcome Obstacles and Win!

Elijah knew he would overcome those turkeys! Why? God told him to do it. How in the world can you fight against God and win? He knows what you don't know about yourself. Let's exercise some wisdom, logic, diplomacy whatever you want to call it. The intelligent way to resolve this without losing too much esteem is to bring out the white flag and surrender. I'm convinced we don't recognize it's him we're fighting against. Once it's realized just give it up.

Elijah knew God was bigger than a false god or an idol. He created everything! Including the false god! Man can't outwit God. God created mind, inventions, techniques, methods, proofs, and cures. They all come from the Creator of life. He gives life to your ideas, let him work for you. He'll give fire to your sacrifice. He'll provide the passion for you to succeed, as long as you don't give up on him. You're a candidate to overcome obstacles and win. Those obstacles give you a testimony. One day you'll look back and thank God you've overcome that issue that's been plaguing you for years. Follow God's order and he'll bring you out victoriously.

> *"And they overcame him by the blood of the Lamb, and by the word of their testimony; and they loved not their lives unto the death."*
> (Revelation 12:11)

God rewards us too. I feel great when I've overcome an issue. That's what service to God is all about. He's a master at drawing the best out of you. It's worth it to surrender your will to his and allow him to give you an overcoming testimony.

The prophets of Baal were without doubt diligent in promoting their cause. In the end, they had no choice but to recognize who has all power.

> *"And when all the people saw it, they fell on their faces: and they said, The LORD, he is the God; the LORD, he is the God."*
> (1 Kings 18: 39)

True worship to the true and living God was restored. Then Elijah rid God's people of the wrong influence, the prophets were slain.

> *"He that overcometh shall inherit all things; and I will be his God, and he shall be my son."* (Revelation 21: 7)

The key is surrendering your will to God's. You can't manipulate and think you'll succeed with him on your terms. Those prophets had to recognize there's destruction in a manmade god, and triumph in the true and living God.

Oh! I'm Prepared

I learned early on in my career that employers want results, not excuses. Don't give them any. Whatever it takes to perform your task, be willing to go the extra mile to perform it well. They have to recognize great performance even when not openly acknowledged. I've had bosses to use my ideas without my knowledge of it. I later found this out. Sometimes others recognize your potential and want to keep you from moving forward. Moving you forward means losing your ideas. Losing your ideas removes the winning edge that's produced by your presence; the presence of God in you.

Prepare yourself for the days to come. Walk today in your role for the future. "Dress for Success." I was taught the person who dresses for success captures the attention of onlookers who are looking for a successor to carry their vision forward.

Become knowledgeable in your field and walk as though you're already there. Not with arrogance, with confidence! The confident person studies! The arrogant person wings it. The confident person enjoys what they're doing. The arrogant is a pretender. The confident person seeks different ways to work solutions. The arrogant thinks *they* are the solution. The confident person is genuine. The arrogant seeks the approval of others for temporary gain.

Prepare yourself for a bright future and you'll stand before kings, perhaps to give them a word from the LORD.

> "And Elijah said unto Ahab, Get thee up, eat and drink; for there is a sound of abundance of rain." (I Kings 18: 41)

Before Elijah's challenge, God was displeased with the ways of King Ahab. Now, King Ahab listened and followed God's instruction. The earth was in a drought for three years as a result of God's displeasure with him. Three years is a long time to be in a famine with nothing growing. All this happened because of idol worship and disobedience. Ahab allowed the wrong influence to affect his walk as a leader.

But the Creator had a way to correct it. He sent Elijah to remove that negative influence. Now the earth could grow and be fruitful again. God's ways prevailed and brought life.

Someone is waiting for your overcoming testimony as you walk honestly with God. "*Study to show yourself approved unto to God.*" (II Timothy 2: 15) You can't dispute facts. Elijah spoke *no rain* and it stopped raining. The altar of sacrifice was drenched three times over with water dripping off of it.

The battle on Mount Carmel was answered by fire that consumed everything, the sacrifice, the water, everything. Then abundance of rain filled the earth again after Elijah spoke. Facts. Know your stuff, it's God working through you.

Professional Standard of Conduct

Mind Your Manners

Questions, Questions, Questions

There is no need to ask questions when you've studied and understand what is acceptable behavior vs. non-acceptable behavior. Become so skilled at what you do, that you are the exception to the rule. Be the Best. Be resourceful. Be professional. There's a code of ethics for governing every profession and abiding in that code grants certain rights, advantages, and privileges.

> *"Sing unto him a new song; play skilfully with a loud noise."*
> (Psalms 33: 3)

The best[4] in a field are individuals who do a specific activity especially well. They devote hours of time by practicing, perfecting, and studying an ability, or an interest to reach a level of competence that exceeds average. They conceptualize in their mind the long-term point of view and that mindset moves them forward. With an increase in concentration and focus, performance increases as they practice. Creating a picture or image, "imaging" of the expected outcome in the mind, increases the ability to realize it. At regular intervals of practice you become skilled and able to maneuver the tools of a chosen activity with expertise and precision. This is a profession.

I've been guilty of asking too many questions, seeking to gain knowledge. Those questions were eventually answered under instruction in a classroom. I found out Education is a tool to realize a dream. Through education you learn the standards of conduct and the rules that govern a profession. Your professional expertise and interactions with others should be extraordinary. It paves your path to take the next step and with that step they'll come looking for you.

---

[4] "What it takes to be Great" http://biz.yahoo.com/weekend/great_1.html

There's a cliché' "the early bird catches the worm." It means [5]*Success comes to those who prepare well and put in effort.* The early bird arrives early, before others. He/she has the best chances of succeeding.

Rising early is also another term for timeliness. Learn the value of time and how it's perceived by the powerful. Timeliness is a key ingredient that stands alone to survival in a professional environment, especially in a culture where everyone is in a hurry and there's a rush to get things done. Americans behave as though they're running out of time, using it up, not valuing it as precious, and quickly dispensing of it. But the reverse is true in other cultures, where people have nothing but time, having it to spare, taking time out for what's important to them, and won't regard timeliness as a priority.

"So teach us to number our days, that we may apply our hearts unto wisdom" (Psalms 90: 12)

Certain values are esteemed differently contingent upon the culture. In Egypt people have nothing but time. In America people are running out of time. A basic understanding of cultural differences and practices is a valuable tool. Priorities, values, and symbols take different meanings from neighborhood to neighborhood, culture to culture. Learning these differences is an indication of a well-rounded individual. Do your homework and take time for understanding others. Mind your manners!

---

[5] http://www.phrases.org.uk/meanings/127000.html

From the Hood to the Good   *Sherry Styles*

You Have A Better Idea

I understand the affliction of God's people. Joseph may have understood it too. Joseph was the son of Israel who became governor of Egypt and saved his family during a 7-year famine. He was gifted with the interpretation of dreams and made a difference in the land of Egypt even in prison. He suffered at the hand of his brothers because of his special giftedness. But oh what a blessing he was!

I grew up in poverty with no aspirations to stay there. Poverty means you don't have much money, it does not mean you are poor. Yesterday, I felt the sentiments of the poor. I know the pain of oppression. Every time you try to rise above your circumstances something happens to keep you down.

I reflected on my childhood when all my friends had money and I had none. I mostly thought of where I am today, relying on the system (unemployment) to support me, working for those with the money who won't allow you to express yourself for fear you'll surpass them, but needing your input all the time. You have a better idea and they know it, but they cannot let you know it.

You don't always have to clean floors and keep house for someone else. You have multi-million dollar ideas that will change the world. Change it. I plan to. I know who I am.

I felt strange and crazy at the time same time although I knew I wasn't. The enemy wanted me to think I was crazy, but God exposed me to this strange craziness so I would understand. I understand the abandoned black women. Yet I'm not really abandoned. She can't give up on her man calling her. She feels the weight of her circumstances and can't move easily even though she's crying out on the inside.

God told me to write although I was hesitant. Now I know why. You're made to think less of yourself in an effort to keep you down, to control you. Your ideas are just as valuable as anyone else, but you have to give them life.

You have a better idea. Don't you Think so?

How You Play the Game - Walk In Authority

> *"Ye are of God, little children, and have overcome them: because greater is he that is in you, than he that is in the world."*
> (1 John 4:4)

Child of God, you are a powerful individual. You have a right to make choices for the outcome of your life. No human being has the right to take that away. God ordained your steps and he has a right to order them. You belong to him and what he says goes. Don't walk around being victimized. Let's take a test to see if you're a victim or a victor.

- A *victor* knows God is in control when he is obeying Gods command, even though it appears another has a winning edge.
- A *victim* thinks others have an unfair advantage.

> *"Many a time have they afflicted me from my youth: yet they have not prevailed against me."* (Psalms 129:2)

Once, a leader over me told me something to do. I knew the authority usurped at this time was an attempt to humiliate me. I obeyed even with this knowledge. God turned it around instantly in my favor and the damage intended was to their detriment not mine.

We are agents employed by God, authorized to act for him on the earth. I am empowered to perform his will, his Word, his purpose. Obedience to God's voice is how you play the game.

> *"For I came down from heaven, not to do mine own will, but the will of him that sent me."* (St. John 6:38)

- A *victor* speaks positively according to God's Word. His conversation is bold and assertive. A definite yes or a definite no! Speaking the outcome and trusting God in the outcome.
- A *victim* speaks passively, in uncertain terms, maybe, possibly, in wonderment about the outcome.

From the Hood to the Good   **Sherry Styles**

> *"But let your communication be, Yea, yea; Nay, nay: for whatsoever is more than these cometh of evil."*   (Matthew 5: 37)

Even when the Hebrew children, Shadrach, Meshach, and Abednigo, faced burning in a fiery furnace, they spoke boldly, saying, *He is able to bring us out!*

> *"If it be so, our **God whom we serve is able to deliver us** from the burning fiery furnace, and He will deliver us out of thine hand, O king."*
>   (Daniel 3: 17)

Abraham was told to sacrifice his only son. Not knowing how God would birth a nation through the promised son, he was certain it would take place even if he did slay his son as a sacrifice. He spoke in faith:

> *"And Abraham said unto his young men, Abide ye here with the ass; and **I and the lad will go yonder and worship, and come again to you.**"*
>   (Genesis 22: 5)

- A *victor* knows his sorrows are temporary. God will make restitution and bring forth deliverance when his purpose is fulfilled. A brighter day is coming as he rests on a promise.
- The *victim* is overcome by sorrow, not at all sure if things will get better, only hoping for a brighter day.

> *"They that sow in tears shall reap in joy."*   (Psalms 126: 5)

- A *victor* speaks how he wants the situation to unfold and leaves the rest to God.
- A *victim* wallows in self-pity, wondering will he do it for me? He tries to figure out how to get it done on his own.

> *"(As it is written, I have made thee a father of many nations,) before him whom he believed, even God, who quickeneth the dead, and calleth those things which be not as though they were."*   (Romans 4:17)

- A *victor* attunes his sight, hearing, taste, touch, and smell to the master's direction. There is only one way to look for the child of God. That way is up!
- The *victim* attunes his sight, hearing, taste, touch, and smell to the things around him, things of the world. He has failed to realize the only way of escape is God.

> *"That your faith should not stand in the wisdom of men, but in the power of God."* (1Corinthians 2:5)

Integrity – Don't Compromise

Integrity is a big word in Christendom. It separates the carnal from the spiritual. It distinguishes lukewarm from cold or hot. It defines those who go all the way, from those who settle for mediocre. *Integrity* is adherence to moral and ethical principles, soundness of moral character, honesty. To a person of integrity, truth is more important than feelings at a time of great adversity.

> *"The just man walketh in his integrity: his children are blessed after him."* (Proverbs 20:7)

Joshua and Caleb were men of great integrity. As leaders chosen to represent their tribes, they were the only two of twelve men who believed God's promise. Although the men in Canaan (The Promised Land) were giants, Joshua and Caleb were not intimidated by them and God delighted in their faith.

> *"But Joshua the son of Nun, which standeth before thee, he shall go in thither: encourage him: for he shall cause Israel to inherit it."* (Deuteronomy 1:38)

Joshua took charge and led the children of Israel to possess the land of promise. He had the right attitude. His greatness was determined by his willingness to stand for truth and God. Perhaps he witnessed the great miracle of the Red Sea parting, whilst the children of Israel crossed it on dry land. Can you imagine how magnificent that was? Just crossing the Miami River is a big feat for us today. To cross a sea of that magnitude would remain etched in my mind throughout eternity. Anytime water and dirt mix, there's mud. God wouldn't even let their toes get wet! What a love! What a God! Joshua placed no limitations on God after this great miracle. He knew better.

His brethren apparently had forgotten what God did to rescue them from the grips of the Pharaoh. They were intimidated by the size of the giants although God already said, *"...Go up and possess it"* (Deuteronomy 1:21)

God knew the giants were there when he gave the promise. The promise was a faith promise. We don't always know his way or method, but as we step into his realm, the faith realm, we develop a trust in him. To launch out in unfamiliar territory is risky business and God seeks such faith. This is where integrity separates believers - the men from the boys.

This is known as *strong in Faith*. We demonstrate strong faith and step out into the unknown where no signs of safety exist. Or, we can hold to what we already know, have experienced, and not move into new territory, not move into the unproven waters. Individuals who step into unproven waters are *strong in Faith*. The patriarch Abraham stepped out and has been indentified as *strong in Faith*. I call these people pioneers of faith. Pioneers are willing to be the exception to the rule, by making new rules. While others ask, *Why me?* Pioneers ask, *Why not me!?*

This is what Peter did. He stepped out on water when he saw Christ walking on water. What boldness of Faith! He was truly a joint-heir. He demonstrated our inheritance in Christ to walk as He walked. By his example, we are children of God indeed. We can do greater works, the sky is the limit, and the unimaginable is possible.

Integrity is at its best during adversity and extreme opposition. It shines brightly. The odds were 2 to 10 that the Israelites could take the land. Joshua and Caleb did not waver, did not back down, and did not change their mind. As a matter of fact their faith became stronger on their journey to the Promised Land. Can you imagine being in the midst of chronic complainers while you're holding to a promise? A lot of negative vibes surrounded these two yet they believed God. I'm certain their moral character had to become strong to resist the temptation. It couldn't have been easy. *Integrity* is the ability to stand for what's right especially when wrong appears right. *Integrity* is a resolution you make within yourself that no one but God has a right to change. It defines your character. Joshua did not compromise his belief and he was rewarded. (Caleb also)

God designated Joshua as leader of the nation of Israel after studying under his leader, Moses. Under Joshua's leadership, the wall of Jericho fell flat and the children of Israel crossed the Jordan River. Such integrity births unique leadership ability. Uncompromising character is what leaders are made of. Courage to stand and declare God's Word is worthy of valor and honor.

> *"Only be thou strong and very courageous, that thou mayest observe to do according to all the law, which Moses my servant commanded thee: turn not from it to the right hand or to the left, that thou mayest prosper withersoever thou goest."* (Joshua 1:7)

Joshua instructed the nation of Israel just how to possess their freedom. Man-made methods won't manifest a God-made promise. The Word of God was a continual guide to success for them. Today the same principle brings salvation, deliverance, and success to God's people. GOD IS CONSISTENT. He won't fail you. (Joshua 1:5) Obedience to his instruction reaps unmatchable rewards.

Give Me MY Mountain!

> *"Hear, O Israel: Thou art to pass over Jordan this day, to go in to possess nations greater and mightier than thyself, cities great and fenced up to heaven, A people great and tall, the children of the Anakims, whom thou knowest, and of whom thou hast heard say, Who can stand before the children of Anak!"* (Deuteronomy 9:1, 2)

You are worth every drop of blood that Jesus paid for your sins. The cost for salvation was extremely high. You are therefore, valuable to God.

God promised to bless the nation of Israel with a perfect plan to get it done. The God of heaven and earth is not like Aladdin. You can't make wishes, rub the magic lamp, and Poof! Wishes come true. God is a provider who listens to you and wants to hear from you. I understand him as a perfect gentleman, who opens doors for you. Blessings await you child of God. Blessings stored up waiting to be unleashed.

> *"A good man leaveth an inheritance to his children's children: and the wealth of the sinner is laid up for the just."* (Proverbs 13: 22)

The Promised Land had inhabitants who were wicked nations. God wasn't pleased with their ways and was driving them out for his names sake. (Deut. 9:4) To get what's rightfully yours may require change. It often does. You must commit yourself to God. A committed heart is the beginning of a beautiful relationship. There's a process to move forward and to take possession of a blessing. Your enemy, the devil, won't just stand by and let God hand it over to you without a fight. Let me explain.

With boldness declare what's rightfully yours by promise of God. You are a joint-heir with Christ.

> *"The Spirit itself beareth witness with our spirit, that we are the children of God: And if children, then heirs; heirs of God, and joint-heirs with Christ; if so be that we suffer with him, that we may be also glorified together."* (Romans 8: 16, 17)

Caleb boldly declared he wanted his land after waiting, enduring, and trusting God for 40 years, with every right to receive it. I can imagine his attitude of gratitude to a God who keeps his promises. I can imagine the determination in his spirit to declare his right to be blessed and tell Joshua to unleash his blessing. He met the conditions and terms of God for his inheritance - *only to Believe*. The omnipotent God has a plan to bless his children. As surely as we take heed to his word, he pours out blessings.

> **"Now therefore give me this mountain**, *whereof the LORD spake in that day; for thou heardest in that day how the Anakims were there, and that the cities were great and fenced: if so be the LORD will be with me, then I shall be able to drive them out, as the LORD said."*
> (Joshua 14:12)

Caleb had a readiness of spirit. If you know anything about sentence structure, then you know the statement above is a declarative statement. (Joshua 14:12) No exclamation point needed, it's not in the passive voice and he asked no questions. However he stated with authority, power, assertively, and assuredly, what he wanted. It was clear he fully expected to receive God's promise.

In today's terms the statement was something like this:

> *Bro you know that deal God made with us back in the day? Now is the time to capitalize on it. I'm ready. I did my part, give me my Mountain! I haven't forgot and now that we have arrived, I want what's coming to me. Man the Dramatics had a song back in the 70's "Hey You Get Off My Mountain!" We gone have to kick some folks out, but I want what's coming to me."*

Can you blame Caleb? He and Joshua paid a price for the ultimate blessing. He was dedicated. He was strong. Are you ready to possess your blessing? The process is what most people don't like. We think we already have it together but God shows what is necessary to change. Joshua and Caleb possessed faith, but were different men after 40 years of walking with God in the wilderness.

A little traveling was necessary to receive the promise, but that's a small price to pay for the ultimate blessing from God. There was more to the process. The first price to pay is waiting on God. If only each of the 12 spies had returned with a good report, the land possession was only a 9-day journey. Did Joshua and Caleb feel let down or frustrated? My guess is yes!

"And Joshua... and Caleb... rent their clothes" (Numbers 14:6)

They believed God, but now had to wait due to a bad report by their brethren. Each man witnessed the goodness of the land when they spied out the land. I believe Joshua and Caleb were in total shock at their brethren's bad report.

The Second price is enduring.

"For the which cause I also suffer these things: nevertheless I am not ashamed: for I know whom I have believed, and am persuaded that he is able to keep that which I have committed unto him against that day."
(2 Timothy 2:12)

Having the ability to reach out and touch your blessing and not have it wasn't easy. People are people wherever you go. The ridicule of those who have no understanding of God and his mysterious ways will toughen your skin. They wanted to stone Joshua and Caleb, but God stopped it. (Number 14:10) The 10 spies' unbelief did not change God.

"For what if some did not believe? shall their unbelief make the faith of God without effect? God forbid: yea, **let God be true, but every man a liar;** *as it is written, That thou mightest be justified in thy sayings, and mightest overcome when thou art judged"*
(Romans 3: 3, 4)

Did they think Caleb was crazy? I believe so. They were despised for holding on to their belief, plagued with negativism. But God would not tolerate it. (Number 14: 27, 28) Caleb and Joshua believed God, so the negativism they suffered reinforced their belief. Throughout the book of Numbers we read where they were journeying to the Promised Land and God gave instruction on what to do once you *"Possess the Land."* Joshua and Caleb witnessed their brethren dying for murmuring against God. God kept his word then too.

God became angry with their chronic complaining and he conversed with Moses about intentions to destroy them. Moses interceded for them and God complied. Stay away from negative people. They can hinder what you think about what God says is true. Unless he says you are strong enough to influence them. He'll always tell you truth.

The Third price is trusting God. As they witnessed the impact of the other spies' negative words, Caleb and Joshua were confident to receive the promise. God kept his word during their journey and their faith was increased. Trusting is a vey important part of faith. A direct path to an ultimate blessing is not always promised but God is faithful to perform his word and will do just as he says.

When God opens a door, there are many adversaries. At first they all appear to be with you, or on your side, even Buddy-Buddy with you. But as you get closer to manifestation of the promise the truth is revealed and you see the covers pulled off.

Your enemy will use many tactics to destroy your faith. Here are three main ones I've encountered. First he'll try to talk you out of it. He realizes how valuable your blessing is. He may want it for himself, or just don't want you to have it. He may not even realize how valuable it is until he sees you with it. So he makes you feel you don't deserve to be blessed, make you talk negatively about it so he can have it, move you out of position. He's just waiting on you to denounce it. Don't give in. Once God has spoken, realize he doesn't make mistakes. Your enemy is subtle and cunning. Just as the serpent tricked Eve, he'll try and trick you.

He doesn't care how he accomplishes his job it's his mission to get you off track. Therefore, the next tactic is he'll try to wear you down. Constantly taunting you and plaguing you with doubt. To *taunt* means to challenge or reproach in a sarcastic, insulting, or jeering manner. People may laugh at you. Make you feel stupid for believing God. Maybe even mock you. To *mock* means to ridicule by mimicry of action or speech. Don't worry God's got you. When someone mocks you, it's really God they're laughing at, the promise originated with him.

"Be not deceived; God is not mocked: for whatsoever a man soweth, that shall he also reap. For he that soweth to his flesh shall of the flesh reap

corruption; but he that soweth to the Spirit shall of the Spirit reap life everlasting." (Galatians 6: 7, 8)

A third tactic is strong delusion. Your enemy will send a substitute, or duplicate, or replica that looks so much like the real thing that you might be mesmerized for a few minutes by how it appeals to you. But don't stay there too long, you don't want to miss God speaking to you. Keep your focus on him at all times. Ain't nothing like the real thing!

Being blessed by God requires change. You'll learn a new language to receive your blessing. The spies observed the inhabitants as giants. A culture unknown to Israel. Remove communication barriers to communicate effectively. Learn to understand the language of the Promised Land. To young people I will learn to speak Hip-Hop. To French heirs I will learn a more sophisticated language. You're entering a new world. Prepare yourself for the chance of a lifetime!

It's time to move! You've been promoted to a higher level. Tell God thanks for considering you. A new opportunity awaits you child of God. A promotion from the Almighty God.

God was sending them to a land of plenty. There are no sorrows with his blessings – only Goodness. A lifetime of goodness. God satisfies every need. A wealthy land with grapes so big they had to carry it between them. (Numbers 13:23) A strong Land flowing with milk and honey, the best fruits of the land. (Numbers 13: 27)

> *"For the LORD thy God bringeth thee into a good land, a land of brooks of water, of fountains and depths that spring out of valleys and hills; A land of wheat, and barley, and vines, and fig trees, and pomegranates; a land of oil olive, and honey; A land wherein thou shalt eat bread without scarceness, thou shalt not lack any thing in it; a land whose stones are iron, and out of whose hills thou mayest dig brass. When thou hast eaten and art full, then thou shalt bless the LORD thy God for the good land which he hath given thee."* (Deuteronomy 8:7-10)

It was abundant, rich, and overflowing with goodness. They were tired of wandering in the wilderness and had much to look forward to. Can I say it again? You have the Victory!

Now speak boldly. Give Me My Mountain!

Walking In It!

Walk in it! Eat it, sleep it, drink it, walk it, talk it, dream it, imagine it. Walk as though it were already. How do you accomplish this? The mindset of the place God is positioning you for must be in your thought processes at all times, at the forefront.

In an undying effort to remain ahead of the game, maintain an awareness of who you are and those around you. You have to go all the way, walking in strict obedience. Those around you know who you are and recognize your value to the kingdom. You must also recognize how valuable you are to the kingdom. Study your environment, study your enemy, and know your God.

Walking in a vision or position requires *insight*. *Insight* is the inward connection to know what's operating around you and how and when it's moving to gain your attention. This is a necessary ingredient to walking with God. It falls right in with Trust. *Insight* is the connection that helps you discern your surroundings.

> "I find then a law, that, when I would do good, evil is present with me"
> (Romans 7: 21)

So then, I ask God to grant me wisdom and maturity to understand how to handle such a wonderful place in him as I walk amongst my brothers and sisters.

As I walk I'm learning information to lead and guide me to the Promised Land. I'm gaining new experiences as I shed the old ones realizing they were seasonal, only to guide me to this place. I rejoice in this walk. It has been ordained by God Almighty. It's a rich place. It's a blessed place. It's a lovely place, I have joy. I have peace. I am Loved. I embrace the process and steps I've taken. A realization enters my thoughts. God placed me on the potter's wheel and personally shaped and formed me into an elaborate vessel on display for his glory. I am as a star shining brightly in the night! I enjoy walking in his goodness.

"O taste and see that the Lore is Good; blessed is the man that trusteth in him." **(Psalms 34: 8)** ☺

A Strong Delusion

A strong delusion will make you believe a lie instead of a truth. Can you imagine someone walking and talking to you everyday, feeding you, clothing you, and caring for you? You would have great respect for them and appreciate everything they've done for you. You should support their every whim.

Now supposing someone else came along with a big smile casting doubt in your mind about the person who took care of you. Wouldn't you say that's a strong delusion, when you know the depths of Love the person has gone through to secure your existence? You know if they'd not been there for you things would have been different.

Under no circumstances should a negative report be received from anyone about them. An illusionist is just as persistent as you are about pursuing your vision. So be wise and understand it's just a strong delusion sent to make you stronger. Stand and remember the Love that covered you when no one else was around. Don't fall for the illusion.

This is what an illusionist does: He watches you, searching for a loophole, or a perceived weakness that he may come in and devour your goods. He's a thief who wants to take your hope, and destroy your joy. He's watching you. Don't move from your place of Authority. Stand on the principles of God.

He's hoping you don't have knowledge. He doesn't want you to gain it then you can't apply it and keep him at bay. No understanding? He tries to block that too. He knows once you gain it you can put him out of business. He wants to keep you confused and walking around in circles. He wants to close your eyes.

He doesn't' realize that the Love of God in your heart will only help promote a move ordained by God to help build God's kingdom.

> *"And for this cause God shall send them strong delusion, that they should believe a lie"*   (I Thessalonians 2: 11)

Raise the Bar

You want to take possession of the ultimate blessing. God wants you to take possession of the ultimate blessing. It's going to require a priestly mentality. Raise the bar in your thinking. You were never meant to be a slave to anyone. You were meant to rule. God liberated and freed the children of Israel from the bondage and rule of taskmasters. Others control you only when you allow it.

> *"And all the children of Israel murmured against Moses and against Aaron: and the whole congregation said unto them, Would God that we had died in the land of Egypt! or would God we had died in this wilderness! And wherefore hath the LORD brought us unto this land, to fall by the sword, that our wives and our children should be a prey? were it not better for us to return into Egypt?"* (Numbers 14: 2, 3)

Why would the children of Israel utter such detestable words? I think most people don't realize the ruling party on earth is not God. We're influenced by leaders, media, family, and friends so much that we talk like them, walk like them, think like them, and won't develop our own true character trying to be imitate them. We don't even realize the control and power others have. Maybe the children of Israel refused to see their bondage as a temporary status until their true value was exposed and ready to break forth. I see it as an experience to bring thanksgiving to God for his fatherly care and concern for them. They were a blessed nation and still are a blessed nation.

> *"Unto him that loved us, and washed us from our sins in his own blood, And hath made us kings and priests unto God and his Father; to him be glory and dominion for ever and ever. Amen"* (Revelation 1: 5, 6)

Kings and priest are leaders. They're the first fruits of the kingdom of God. Why settle for second best when God ordained his best for you? We settle for less when we've encountered a few bumps in the road to tide us over. Not realizing it wasn't intended by God as a permanent situation. We settle for less when we don't wait on God to move or answer us. The best is greater than what you imagine. His thinking is higher than ours. His wisdom is infinite.

When I know he promised the best, I'll expect it. Society tries to dictate who we are but I can't bow down to a preconceived idea about me and walk in that. I was designed to walk in Love (Ephesians 5:2)
I was designed to be free (St. John 8:36) I was designed to walk in the image of God. (Genesis 1: 26, 27)

> *"All the best of the oil, and all the best of the wine, and of the wheat, the firstfruits of them which they shall offer unto the LORD, them have I given thee."* (Numbers 18: 12)

When the temple was in preparation for building, the materials King David gathered for its construction were abundantly supplied. This was a representation of a place to worship the creator of the universe. God doesn't want a shabby dwelling place. He wants splendor, state-of-the-art technology and materials. He wants skilled workmen, cunning in building their craft for every manner of work in God's house. The building was constructed so precisely, so methodically that *"neither hammer nor axe nor any tool of iron heard in the house, while it was in building"* (1 Kings 6:7)

> *"And David said, Solomon my son is young and tender,* **and the house that is to be builded for the LORD must be exceeding magnifical, of fame and of glory throughout all countries:** *I will therefore now make preparation for it. So David prepared abundantly before his death."* (1 Chronicles 22: 5)

He's secured a mansion in heaven for you with streets of gold. The walls are of the finest precious stones: jasper, sapphire, chalcedony, emerald, and others. The gold there is like nothing on earth. It is transparent like clear glass. Give him your best. Your Praize to God is no shabby second hand Praize. Give him your finest! He deserves it. You were designed to Praize an awesome God.

He made agreements with Solomon after he constructed the building:

"And the word of the LORD came to Solomon, saying, Concerning this house which thou art in building, if thou wilt walk in my statutes, and execute my judgments, and keep all my commandments to walk in them; then will I perform my word with thee, which I spake unto David thy father." (1 Kings 6: 11, 12)

God wants to covenant with you.

Dreams Don't Die, But They Do Take Time

Behold the beauty of a platinum wedding running smoothly with everything in place. To share in the joy of the beginning of a marvelous night. Only a replica of the beauty and joy of a life to come.

Cinderella, the bride. The story of one who dares to dream in a hateful world. And then her dreams come true. Now in a palace, the one who swept the cinders of a chimney?

The business behind all the Beauty takes careful planning. Others see the beauty but don't see the effort to make it all come true.

There are times in life that we dream Big Dreams and they're so real that we have the taste and flavor in our mouth. So real that you see yourself there at every waking moment. So real you can reach out and touch it. You are really there. Then you wake up. And then life's toils and snares attempt to blow out the candle on your dreams. How dare you!

But God says "Don't give up on your dreams because Dreams Take Time." Precise Planning. Dotting every i and crossing every t. For synchronized timing everything falls into place. And it's Beautiful!

Dreams only die when you give up on them. Only when you say ashes to ashes, dust to dust.

It took two days – 2,000 years, for the fulfillment of Gods dream, to save his people from their sins. He strategically planned how he would come into the world and where he would come. He articulated so beautifully a simple plan to redeem mankind. And he plans strategically to engraft each one of us into his plan. He planned the date, time, and circumstances to draw you close to him. Only he didn't start planning it a month before your heart was changed. No, from your birth he knew how to draw you to him. He knew what path you would take and what path would lead you to him. He charted your course.

His dream to save you did not happen over night. He knew you were his from the beginning. Toils, snares come to discourage you from grasping hold of the beauty of Salvation. It's yours.

The snares come to distract you into believing your dream won't come true. Cancel that assignment because God does not give a dream and snatch it away!

"I had fainted, unless I had believed to see the goodness of the LORD in the land of the living." (Psalms 27: 13)

God gave the dream that you might live until it is fulfilled. Cast away your cares and doubts for it shall surely come to pass.

"For the vision is yet for an appointed time, but at the end it shall speak, and not lie: though it tarry, wait for it; because it will surely come, it will not tarry." (Habakkuk 2:3)

And it will be Marvelous!

"Behold ye among the heathen, and regard, and wonder marvelously: for I will work a work in your days which ye will not believe, though it be told you." **(Habakkuk 1:5)**

The Test

As promised, I mentioned at the beginning there would be a simple test to help you remember the three principles. Whenever you face stress or opposition in a foreign environment you must take immediate action to control the situation. Assert yourself, it sends a strong message. Then perform an awareness check. Follow this method for successful results, it works every time!

Take a minute to recognize what's really happening. Ask yourself these questions:

Where am I?

Who am I dealing with?

How do they operate?

Chances are, you have not considered these three questions and you can reduce any stress instantly.

An example of this is quite appropriate at this time.

Earlier I shared an experience regarding work, when my supervisor claims she didn't receive the report I left on her desk in her In-box. I know she received it, but somehow it just disappeared. I did not get angry about it at all.

I resolved the situation in my mind as follows:
I know where I am: I am not at home, I am at a place of business, a professional environment.
I know who I'm dealing with: A supervisor, who wants results not excuses, a woman in management, a person very efficient and precise in managing a department.
I know how they operate: This could be a test of wills and competency. The boss is the boss. Even if she had the report, she could handle this matter any way she wanted to.

I already knew the possibility existed of a missing report. It could happen at any time, which is why I made copies in the first place. Therefore, I handled myself professionally and was prepared by returning to my work area and producing a copy of the original report.

The original report was placed on her desk by me. I really doubted if the report was lost, by the efficient way she conducted herself. She was very precise in her operations. There was no reason was for me to get upset about an incident I already had a solution for. In this business environment, with a supervisor, who is a professional and conducts business with accuracy, my behavior is to respond in like manner.

My transition *From the Hood to the Good* has been great. I learned three principles, I gained confidence in my God, and I learned how to walk in a foreign environment.

Conclusion

Finally, I was encouraged to walk in my newfound destiny. No longer am I captive to the Hood, but the Good shines through at every waking moment and I'm rather excited about it.

My Three Rules of the Hood motivated me to share information locked within my heart. It gave me confidence knowing who I am and how to conduct myself around others. As I began to make a transition and understand how different cultures operate, I learned how important the Good is. The Good comes from God and makes a difference everywhere you go.

Is the Good waiting to break forth in you? Please take the time to walk in it! You owe it to yourself to experience the Ultimate Blessing.

Books By Sherry Styles

From the Hood to The Good
Good Advice – Work, stay employed, without collapsing

Surviving a Crisis – Without Emotion?
Help me!

Soon to Come!
The Need for 21st CENTURY EVANGELISM in the Apostolic Church
Action – Let's follow our call.

Victory Inspirations to Motivate You to ACTION!
Poetry – You can Make it!

Sweet Plague
Romance – Love is worth waiting for.

www.ingramcontent.com/pod-product-compliance
Lightning Source LLC
Chambersburg PA
CBHW060356050426
42449CB00009B/1757